To: My S
John Patrick Mingo...

MAY GOD KEEP YOU
Always close to HIM

Queen Mother
Dr. Delois Blakely

JAN 19, 2015
MLK DAY
My Little Angel
INI-Chinwa

The Harlem Street Nun

Dr. Delois Blakely

Dedicated to Bumpy Johnson, the Godfather of Harlem, who taught the Harlem Nun the way of the streets and her way through the streets after leaving the convent.
In Memory of Chinua Achebe (Author of Things Fall Apart), the giant of manifesting thought, vision and experiences in the literary world. Thank you for speaking truth to power.

Copyright © 1987 Delois Blakely ISBN 978492289678
Copyright © 2013 Early Edition Delois Blakely
All Rights Reserved to New Future Foundation Inc.
Qiyamah Abdallah from Tree of Touba publishing for formatting my book
with New Future Foundation Inc..
Edited by Cecelia Adams, The Gentlewomen Publishing
*No part of this publication shall be used without the expressed written
permission of the Author. All academic reasons must express written
permission to the Author.

Introduction

(This is the TRUE STORY of Sister Act)

The purpose of this book is to hold on to your innate gifts that God has endowed you with. Creative energy comes from the Creator; let no man rob you of your inspirations, your reflections and your spiritual awakening that only the Creator can endow you. There are those that want to abuse, snatch, rape, pillage, exploit and annihilate your gifts. They will do anything in their power to silence you from claiming what is rightfully yours. No one has a right to dehumanize you in your mystical and sacred space because you are destined to be here. Divine Gifts must be cherished from a force that is the beginning and the end of all things. Your soul energy is the energy that guides and leads you throughout time. I call on all of us to cherish our culture, our traditions, our spirit and heritage in a healing that is unrecognized by the forces of mankind. Let us live in the moment of the universe. Love of our universe and peace, love and harmony that balances the scale of justice. As the mountains bow to the valley and as the rivers and the lakes flow in silence as a lagoon, blessings to all as I share the memories of my life that has been granted to me as I pass through.

Blessings, Queen Mother Dr. Delois Blakely

Acknowledgements

There are several people who encouraged me and supported me in telling my stories. I would personally like to thank the following people for editing, proof reading, recording, typing and listening to my stories with great laughter : Claude Brown(Man Child and the Promise Land) , Marie Brown Associates, Dr. John Cardwell, Jean Green, Frank Harris, Patricia A. Ettrick, John O'Neill, Dr. Lawrence Kasdon, Attorney George Hammond, Barbara Whyte, Carolyn Jenkins, Babatunde Harrison, Deadria Farmer Paellmann-Restitution Study Group, Mohamed Fofanah, Kenneth Amanze proof reader, Robert Santiago, New Future Foundation, Inc. Honorable Mention Emeritus: Attorney Morris Ernst, Hon. William H. Booth, Dr. David Barry- New York City Mission Society, Clifton Glover, Congresswoman Shirley Chisholm, Dr. Doxey Wilkerson, Yvonne Easton, Virginia Lee (NFF Student), Bertha Klausner International Literary Agent. I would also like to acknowledge the many college students from New York University (NYU), Yeshiva, and Columbia University that worked for New Future Foundation Inc. that participated in this process over the last 40 years, special thanks to student Michael Goodwin from City College(CUNY) of Harlem New York City. The White House under President Jimmy Carter gave me the opportunity to serve on the "U.S. Commission for the International Year of the Child 1979" studying issues, policies, legislations and programs that affected the lives of 66.5 million youth under the age of 18 years old. I acknowledge two (2) of my favorite Popes in the Catholic Church that inspired me in caring for the sick, the poor and the less fortunate in our society as well as the youth, Pope John XXIII and Pope John Paul II. I had the privilege of meeting Pope John Paul II at the United Nations during his first trip to the United Stated. This body of work was also inspired by the Franciscan Handmaids of the Most Pure Heart of Mary Order. (FHM) Convent.

Table of Contents:

Chapter One: Roots

I am not in search of my roots nor am I in doubt of my identity. I know myself; look at my features. Look at my face and you will share my conviction. My face is on the sphinx; my ancestors have given me the spirit of rest about my identity.

When I soldiered into Ghana, my ancestors captured me and would not allow me to leave. I went to the airport to depart for other West African countries but my name mysteriously disappeared from the computer, it could not be traced. I was restless for a week in Ghana, I was in Accra. When I realized that there was no way for me to leave I went back to the house I was staying in with the other elders of the community. I cried. I wept and moaned my fate like a baby.

The elders of the house I was staying in said that they felt the spirit of my ancestors surrounding me and that the ancestors did not want me to leave but I was still restless and that disturbed them. I was advised to go to the seaside and relax and that I did, to meditated. I looked at the ocean waves billow at high velocities toward me, "Why can't I leave Ghana?" I asked myself. I had a plane ticket but the computer at the airport did not show that I had entered the country. *Why? Why couldn't I leave?*

As the sun retreated into its cocoon to give way to the descending dusk I was still on the beach. I walked up and down the shoreline and as the waves splashed occasionally at my feet I contemplated the mystery of my circumstances. Was there something wrong with the computer at the airport? Was something wrong with the manager of the traveling agency? Did they misspell my name? Was someone trying to toy with my fate? Did *I* do anything wrong? Will I ever be able to leave Ghana? I just pondered over and over.

I reminded Charlie, the brother at the travel agency in Ghana, he must have made a mistake. I suggested that he call New York but the agents there could not give me any answers. "Who is holding me here?" I asked myself. As I left the seaside to return to the house where I was staying, a picture of sadness covered me. I was unhappy. A female elder wanted to comfort me and I asked her why I felt the way I did. She told me that it was important for me to go to Cape Coast Castle. The elder said that I had to make the journey I was trying to avoid.

The next day I set out on a dirt road to the Cape Coast Castle. As the driver navigated the bumpy and dusty road, I sat there, thinking about my fate. I discovered that there was a secret urge within me to get to the castle as fast as I could. The anxiety grew to a level at which I wished someone or something would catapult me to the castle. I wanted to get there for a reason I did not understand but which I later discovered to be the hands of my ancestors. They communed with my spirit. They wanted to have me around for reasons best known to them but all the way from the United States? What exactly did they want from me?

As we drove on it seemed as if it were taking longer and longer to arrive at out destination. I spoke to the driver about the way I was feeling. I wanted to be sure that I was not daydreaming. I wanted to be sure this experience was happening on a physical level and not in the metaphysical realm. But the driver, a thin man in his thirties appeared to be immersed in his own thoughts. His job, to drive and to provide security for me he did well. However it seemed that anything else he didn't know or didn't care to know. His responses to my questions were unintelligible. The Pidgin English he spoke was probably a factor. It dawned on me then that on this trip I was alone.

When I arrived in the town that the driver took me to some government officials were waiting to accompany me down to Cape Coast. The town called Elmina was very ancient and served as the headquarters of a local government. In the American governmental system the town would be considered a county. We found our way to the mayor's office where there were evident signs of my expectation. The mayor was glad to receive me and acknowledged receiving the message sent ahead by the government informing him of my coming. He told me to relax because we would be setting off for the Cape Coast later. But I was not sure I wanted to relax. Instead I stressed the need to go there quickly. The mayor did not understand my sense of urgency and was at a loss as to why I had to be there immediately. I kept pestering him but he insisted on me sitting down for a few minutes while he prepared to join me on the journey to the Cape Coast.

I was given the instruction to put on 'tie and dye', a type of dress called *kampala* or *adire*, native to parts of West Africa. I was required to remove what I was wearing and put on the traditional clothing including a pair of shoes. With these instructions I informed the mayor who quickly arranged to get all of the necessities. I expected to get to the Cape Coast by noon. I told the mayor that I had to go soon; he was still at a loss as to why I was so anxious. I could not explain it either. I said to the mayor that he could take his time and I would meet him later.

My eyes were literally fixed on the wristwatch as I instructed the driver to be at the castle by noon. I had previously asked the guards in the mayor's office how long it would take to get there and they assured me that it would not be long. I urged the driver to speed as much as he could so that we could get there on time. He hurriedly drove understanding my sense of urgency but he made several mistakes on the directions that I gave. "Ask people if you missed your way we've got no time to waste," I said. "We have to be there on time and please, move faster", were my pestering words. The driver, like other African males, was unaccustomed to taking orders from a woman. He was embarrassed as I dished out my instructions. I could see that he did not like it. To him, it was emasculating but I could not help it. I had received my instructions and I intended to fulfill them.

I told the driver again and again to stop and ask for directions to the castle. Reluctantly, he stopped and was told to go this way and that. Unsatisfied, I ordered him to stop once more at which point I spotted a young man walking by. "Young man" I called out of the window of the car, "Please help me. I'm trying to get to the Cape Coast Castle." The young man looked behind him in the direction of the voice. He did not glance at the driver but directly at me sitting in the back of the car. "I was going to the Cape Coast Castle" he said. And with that, he got into the front seat of the car, turned around and stared into my face without saying a word.

The young man took us straight to the castle and when we arrived he got out of the car and began to walk away without allowing me the chance to express my appreciation. I even wanted to give him some money for his assistance but he refused. He just left without introducing himself which I felt was a little strange. At a little distance he glanced back at me but what perplexed me the most was that I never saw him again, in or around the castle. It was almost as if he vanished. I will never forget that young man, his face which is emblazoned in my memory: pleasant features…a dark, smooth face as round as the moon.

I jumped out of the car and rushed into the castle. I was told to take off my shoes and put on my sandals. I carried the tie-dye clothes into the first shed within the castle and changed into them. I carried some bottled water with me. Some of the men working in the castle were startled when they saw me arrive unaccompanied. Obviously the police had been ahead of me and had informed them of my coming. But they also expected to see the mayor and here I was alone. My arrival elicited a flurry of excitement as the men started asking amongst themselves, "Where is the mayor?" "Is he not here?" "What happened?" They conversed with each other because they were informed that I would stay overnight in the castle and they kept stepping out of their work area to see who I was. I on the other hand, spoke to no one. I just went straight down the corridor seeking the way into the dungeon.

As I walked I saw an elder dressed in long garb common with Muslims. He wore a small white cap and held a prayer rug which he laid on the ground. He was preparing for prayers as I observed him kneel on the rug. I stood at a fairly long distance away as to not disturb him and watched as he prayed. When he completed his prayer I approached him and asked him the way to the dungeon. He pointed out the dungeon for women, there was another for men.

I entered the one for women. It was a dark place, lit only by the rays of light that shone through the door courtesy of the midday sun. The stairs descending from the entrance were about two and a half feet apart. It was like jumping every time I took a step. The further I went down the more the darkness enveloped me. I became numb; my body felt as if it were no longer mine. I kept going deeper into the dungeon and as I did, I breathed a foul stench. An eerie, nasty suffocation blanketed me as my hand piloted my way deeper into the dungeon using the walls for guidance. Then all the horrors imaginable permeated my consciousness, I began to wail and my body began to vibrate. For stability I presses against the wall and moved on carefully. I saw a glow in the distance and as I moved closer I discovered an altar on which there were lit candles.

Just then the reality of my surroundings hit me as the horrors of the past became palpable in the present. There were intermittent splashes on the walls from the rolling ocean waves which woefully failed to wash away the five-hundred year old stench. The dungeons were built in a sadistic manner, making it impossible for those held therein to squat or even bend to touch their knees. Slaves were expected to stand as long as they remained there, laden with heavy chains tied to one another. Excreta were done while standing adding to the stench five hundred years of sea waves could not wash away.

I could not but ask God at that moment "why?" Why did you allow this to happen to my ancestors? Why did you allow this gravity of man's inhumanity to his fellow man? Why did you make it possible for one man to reduce another to a beastly state? *Why, why, why?* I repeatedly asked the questions but God was not to provide me with the immediate answers that I desired. Perhaps he was just watching me for now, withholding his revelations.

Then, my heart went out to Adam Blakely, my great-grand father. He had experienced the horrors of this dungeon. It could not have been in a dream, the evidence was there staring at me as I stood there ruminating. I pondered, "What might Adam Blakely have gone through?" He had survived the voyage to the dungeon and was then shipped to the Carolinas in the United States of America. There and then, it dawned on me how strong Adam Blakely must have been to have survived those tribulations. I soon came to realize why and how he survived on the plantation; a combination of awe inspiring emotional, physiological, psychological, and most importantly, spiritual strength.

I was born on October 1, 1941 to James Blakely Jr. and Margarita Blakely in Florida at Fort Lauderdale; my father had migrated there from Montgomery Alabama. His father, James Blakely Sr., married a Native American woman simply called Lizzy, the features of whom my father greatly shared. My grandfather was the last of seventeen children of his father, Adam Blakely. My mother, Margarita, was an African American of the Caribbean extraction whose parents resided there. My father, the eldest of three, had five children with my mother, all girls. Jimmy-Lee, born in

1939, myself in 1941, Doris in 1942, Jacquelyn in 1943 and Juanita in 1944.

The memories of my mother, though fading, remain with me. I remember her as a short woman with short hair and large hoop earrings. My mother, a black woman with short hair and strong African features. Not a fat woman, about 5'4" in height she was called "high" meaning that she was from the Caribbean, but I think she was from the Carolinas, the Deep South. I never knew any of my mother's relatives. What I do know I learned from my father, though he never talked about my mother's family and we never visited any of her relatives. When my sisters and I got older we tried to piece together some history of our mother. We concluded Daddy and her met while he was traveling. They liked each other and were help mates. When Jimmy-Lee was conceived they settled for family life.

My mother always stayed at home when my father went to work. I was a very sickly child which gave me the opportunity to spend a lot of time with her. She never spanked me; in fact she did not want to have anything to do with disciplining me. I used to suck on my fingers and instead of my mother stopping me she took me to a woman who tried to scare me into abandoning the habit. I was able to express myself without any fear of reprimand. My mother let me dress in her clothes and walk around the house pretending to be older. She was always there for me anytime I wanted her.

I remember when I was taken to school I did not like it; I did not want to go. I cried so much that my mother bought me candy to assuage my protests. I had a very close relationship with my mother; she was my soul mate, my playmate and my best friend. The only time my mother and I were apart was when I had to be admitted to Dr. Sistrunk's clinic. That was my second house. Doctor Sistrunk was so nice that the clinic was the only place I would go without protest and be fine without my mother being there with me. The nurse in the clinic was also very nice and she always made my stay exciting.

Although my mother allowed me to be myself, she stopped me from being the active, explorative and the talkative child that I was. Her conversations with me were more or less functional; calling me when it was time to eat or asking about my health. My health was not only important to my parents but to my neighbors as well. People would come over and bring me coloring books, crayons and anything else that they felt necessary to help the little patient who had to stay home. When I went to the hospital, everyone knew about it and I received everyone's sympathy. I became a celebrity between all of the attention I got from my mother and my neighbors.

I was closest to my father like a brother and a friend because he was more demonstrative with his affection. He was more indulging, always with a hearty laugh. I would wait anxiously for him to turn the corner when I watched for him at the window. The day began when he came into the house from work after that I could be put to bed and sleep contently. My father and I naturally grew closer when my mother died giving birth to my youngest sister. I remember when my mother was pregnant with my youngest sister. She always liked to eat crackers and cheese. For a long time, I thought that eating crackers and cheese gave you a baby. Her stomach got big and I did not want that to happen to me. To this day I don't think my parents ever realized why I would not eat cheese and crackers. I ate pickles instead. Now, I basically had my father to myself, my sisters were no competition; my asthma always triggered his sympathy and affection.

Chapter Two: Mamma's Death

"It's so sad," I heard a lady say.

Even though they talked softly, I could still hear voices drifting down the hall past the bathroom to the bedroom I shared with Jimmy-Lee Doris and Jacqueline. I think the person who was talking was Miss Ruth, a neighbor, who lived on the other side of the hedge that separated our neighboring houses. Ours was the white wooden house with green trimming. It was one story like a bungalow with a screened front porch, a dining room and a kitchen in a large space separated by a banister with a living room, bath and a back porch. This was only on one side of the house the other side off of a long hall was the enclosed porch and three bedrooms. One thing I can say about that house is that many changes in life, mine and others, happened there.

"It happens so often but each time it's sadder when the children are so young", said another voice, "She just had her children too fast- the youngest is just nine months old….Even though Jimmy is a wonderful father-you couldn't ask for a better one, it seems like all the odds are against little girls with no mother."

That voice I was sure belonged to Miss Lillie Mae from across the street. Miss Lillie Mae was Lucille's mother. Lucille was my favorite playmate. She was like my sister. Jimmy-Lee was always outside so I didn't have her to keep me company until we were at the table eating or in bed. Since I was usually confined to the house Jimmy-Lee and I did not develop a close relationship when we were younger. Unlike other older sisters she was not forced to drag her younger sisters around. Lucille never minded playing indoors with me since I was not allowed to go outside and play in the yard or on the sidewalk. I didn't know any of the games the kids played outside but Lucille was content playing 'house' and 'school' with me. If I was caught outside even for a minute, Miss Ruth, Miss Lillie, Miss Mae, or any other grownup in the neighborhood would scold me. I was made to either go back inside or accompany them back to their house. I learned a lot about people and families in my neighborhood. Usually, what was lacking in my own family I enjoyed in someone else's.

I wondered why Miss Ruth and Miss Lillie Mae were still in our house. They were here last night too. Did they spend the night? So many people from the neighborhood had come to my house last night to sit and whisper. I was used to other people being in our house because there were times when my family took in people as roomers or people who needed a place to stay. But we didn't have anyone with us now. *Where is my daddy?* I thought to myself. *My mother is in the hospital to have another baby, where is my daddy?*

We girls were in bed but I think I was the only one awake. I still heard the talking down the hall and I decided to pretend I was asleep so I could hear more.

"How is Jimmy going to manage now with these girls and the household?" Miss Lillie Mae inquired. They were talking about my father now. Miss Ruth tried to say something but her voice was caught by a sob. I stayed quiet and tried to figure out what was going on.

"I'll start getting the girls washed up and dressed Miss Ruth, if you'll prepare their breakfast. Or, if you'd like, you can get the girls washed and dressed and I'll see to the breakfast. Which ever you want is fine with me," said Miss Lillie Mae.

"I'll go back and see to the girls," said Miss Ruth. "If you need anything for breakfast let me know. I have some breakfast food at home that I can bring over."

"I already looked in their icebox," said Miss Lillie Mae, "and there is plenty in there. You know how Jimmy is about having plenty of food in the ice box...it's just so sad what happened."

I heard Miss Ruth approach the bedroom hall and take a deep breath before walking down the hall to where our room was. I closed my eyes just enough so I could appear to be asleep but see what she was up to. When Miss Ruth appeared in our doorway she looked from one sleeping girl to the next shaking her head sadly. In her arms she carried what looked like dresses and some bags from a store downtown. I had never seen those things before. Still with my eyes closed and my neck craned up slightly to see what was happening, I observed Miss Ruth place on the foot of Doris's bed four of the prettiest dresses I had ever seen. They were all different sizes. The one that looked like it would fit me was white with fairy tale ruffles around the neck and the hem with a wide satin sash. It looked like the kind of dress a princess would wear when she was going to a castle ball with her prince. It was so beautiful I didn't want to but I couldn't help but wonder if it were for m…"No" I said. I wouldn't even think about it just in case.

Miss Ruth went back to the living room and came back with a stack of four shoe boxes. Out of the Shoe Boxes she took four pairs of shiny white shoes and placed them neatly on the dresser. I could see that one pair would fit me. She rustled inside of the bags and took out four pairs of white socks and placed them on the dresser too. The dresses on the bed, the shoes, and the socks on the dresser had all of the attention I could give without being discovered awake. I was afraid to be fully awake in case this was a dream and the pretty dresses, socks, and shoes would disappear. A prince would be proud to take me in his carriage pulled by white horses. I looked from the dresses to the shoes. As I said they were shiny; white with white silk bows. The socks had little white dots all over them and ruffle at the tops.

Ever since my mother had gone to the hospital to have the baby, Miss Ruth and Miss Lillie Mae had come to our house to help cook and feed us and get us ready for school. They helped dress us and took some of our clothes to their homes to be washed and brought back clean and smooth. I remember my mother had been in the hospital for many days and yesterday, almost everyone in our neighborhood came to our house to hug us girls and daddy. Why they came I did not know at the time. Why they were so sad I didn't know either.

I was still spying the princess dress when Miss Ruth turned toward where I was pretending to be asleep.

"Tinky, Tinky, are you awake?"

I can not pin point when it started nor can I explain why but "Tinky" was me. A name I responded to from my earliest remembrance. I pretended to wake up, still not taking my eyes off of the princess dress. Miss Ruth helped me out of my pajamas and into my robe. As she pulled the pajama top over my head I struggled to get it off so I could get back to gazing at the princess dress. She led me to the bathroom as I twisted my head back toward the dress, just

everyone was so sad I was going to the ball.

My sisters, my father, Miss Ruth, Miss Lillie Mae and I went out onto the porch. Around the porch, on the porch, on the sidewalk, and the street was practically everyone in the neighborhood. They watched as my family approached a long shiny black car. As soon as I got near the car a young man appeared, handsomely dressed in a black suit and tie. He smiled at me and opened the door. He gave me a nod as if he knew who I was and where I was going. My father and sisters got in with me. The other ladies, neighbors and distant relatives got into other cars. Slowly we drove down the street with everyone in the neighborhood out to see us go. I waved as I went by. My father watched as we rode to the castle in the long black car. He had always known I had an active imagination because he always talked to me about reality. He said in reality my sisters and I would have to make a lot of adjustments, he told us a tragedy had occurred. This was not a fairy tale after all.

In the car my father tried to explain that our mother had died and would not be coming back to our house. He said that her body was in the car in front of the one we were riding in. After we left the funeral parlor, we took her to the cemetery where she was lowered into her grave. I was sad my mother could not go to the ball. I was only four years old.

I really did not understand the impact of the funeral. I remember the mount olive church as white and my mother lying in a casket. I remember seeing my father cry. At the church he raised us up so that we could see mamma. At the cemetery he had all of us put a flower on her grave. I wanted to keep my flower to take it to the ball but, daddy made me throw it into the hole.

After the funeral we went to our house first. A lot of people were there who wanted to hug us and feed us. After we left the house, my father, my sisters, and myself went to a restaurant. The next day my father left us at some strange lady's house. It was my first time being dropped off somewhere other than at home. My father felt he could not keep the house. It was his intention to finally buy it but with mama gone, it changed the plans.

Chapter Three: Children at Play

Miss Geneva (we kids called her Big Fat Geneva) had a nursery school in the basement of the Mount Calvary Baptist Church where every parent wanted their children to attend. It seemed as if Big Fat Geneva had a way with children and getting them to learn. When the children left Big Fat Geneva, they were well prepared for kindergarten and first grade. Unfortunately, things got off to a bad start for me.

On the very first day I was to start at Big Fat Geneva's, my mother bought me an ice cream cone to try and smooth over the pain of my separation from her. When I arrived at the nursery school, I clung to that ice cream. It was not really the ice cream cone that was important to me- all my sisters will tell you that desserts and sweets weren't my thing. They used to practically line up to get my dessert after supper, knowing that more than likely I was going to give it away. It was the principle of it all. My mother was trying to placate me, a little girl who had spent most of her life indoors or in the hospital. Didn't Big Fat Geneva take that cone away from me? You would think she would be sensitive and sympathetic towards a young child who was clearly anxious about the whole affair. Oh no, not her. She was a no nonsense teacher who got her way with the children and the parents. I supposed that's how she coerced the little children into learning their lessons. But I am telling you that her teaching style did nothing to help me love school.

When I was in the first grade, my active imagination had not lessened. I was a dreamer even then. I wanted to experience life gracefully and peacefully, but schools were not easy going places because I found that schools punished me for the things I liked to do. Teachers did not understand that children could learn in more than one way. For example, one day I was a little late returning to the classroom. When we went to recess, I had gone directly to the merry-go-round. I thought that the merry-go-round was one of the best things about school, I loved it. I even practiced my counting by counting the nails on the seat of the merry-go-round. When I rode it all of the hard details of life melted into a soft blur. If I concentrated hard enough all the things I saw were transformed into other things and places. I could imagine strange and wonderful visions as I spun around and around. I think the merry-go-round must have been addictive. I knew I was later returning to class but somehow, for that merry-go-round I was willing to suffer the consequences.

When recess ended that day I decided that I would stay on the merry-go-round. I preferred the view of life that went 'round and 'round to the static painful regimentation of the classroom. Sure enough when I entered the classroom, the teacher was ready with her paddle and slapped me solidly on the palms of my hands. That did it. All of the rebelliousness I inherited from my father reared up. I must have said some nasty things back to her because for the rest of the year our relationship was not better than a barely peaceful existence. I knew then I was never going to give much to school. I was stubborn like my father and perhaps a bit contrary to boot. It wasn't until the third grade that I came to terms with the repetitive and predictable routines of school.

When I was six going on seven, it was only in the summer that I would be allowed to go outside. Beyond our back porch was a wide area which extended the length of the block and which if it had been paved, would be a road big enough to accommodate two cars. It was in this area that some of the neighborhood boys built a house out of wood big enough for several of us to fit in. It had a flat top for a ceiling; we had to bend down to go inside and avoid bumping our heads on the ceiling. My sisters Juanita and Doris played "house" along with, Clotil and Patricia from down the street, and the twins Claudette and Claude from across the street. We also played with "quiet Lorraine," and her younger sister Merdi. Rudy and Sherman sometimes played with us as well. I would always be the mother. They had no problem with me being the mother because they liked the way I played the role. I listened to all their stories and I provided justice equally to all my children.

Once in a while when we played "house," Rudy was good to Sherman but, he would pick on the girls or stick his tongue out at them. They all knew that I was a fair mother and I would spank anyone who did not treat another fairly. I was good to them and I cared about them; none of the children behaved badly. They would say, "Yes, Mamma" to whatever I had to tell them. While the children played I would go inside the house and clean, getting it ready for their return. I arranged furniture, put table cloths on the dining table, and arranged whatever dolls we had. I called in the children for lunchtime and sometimes I would have to scold them loudly to come down out of the mango tree. I served the children peanut butter and jelly or cheese sandwiches. Supper was always arranged nicely on the table, a crate covered with cloth; our chairs were small boxes. Flowers from our neighbors' yards were put in jars and bottles adding a special detail to our house.

When all of us would sit down to eat, I would ask the children what they had done that day. The children would tell me what they had done and any problems that had arisen among them. Some days they all complained that Claude would not let them go up the mango tree or that one of them was hit by another. In these cases I would scold my children about not playing nicely together. I asked them why they had problems playing with each other and most of the time, the boys wanted to do something different from the girls. Other times it was because the boys would tease the girls. After they ate, the children would ask me if they could go back outside and I would tell them, "yes, until your daddy comes home." When their daddy, Claude would come inside, (Sherman was too young to play daddy) the children would come in to have dinner. When they all came I would clean up the kitchen and start preparing dinner. Dinner was mud pies and I would have to leave the house to make them. I always made them next to running water. They would stay in the sun to bake and would be garnished in different ways, each becoming a completely different dish. I cut the pies with the knife I made out of a stick.

When Daddy came into the house I would kiss daddy on the cheek and take his shoes off. Daddy got to sit in the big chair. I would ask daddy how his day was at work and he would say that he had a rough day. He would tell me stories about the people on his job and that he enjoyed the lunch I packed for him. I told the daddy which child had misbehaved and he would promise to reprimand the offending child after dinner. When dinner was ready, I called the children in one by one to wash their hands and faces and take a seat in their own chairs at the table. When everyone was seated at the table we would bow our heads and the daddy would say a prayer. I would insist upon the children eating their spinach. I made sure the children ate their vegetables before they could drink any lemonade or Kool-Aid. You know how children can be. Once they swilled their

Kool-Aid they would be too full to eat anymore. But when the children ate properly, they would always seek the approval from daddy.

After dinner was finished we had a little family talk. I would let them stay up a little while and remind them they had school in the morning and that they would have to get ready for bed. I saw to it that they all took baths. I made sure Rudy was the last one so that the other children had a chance to get in their beds and go to sleep. This also gave Rudy a chance to talk with his father. We had bunk beds in two separate rooms, one for the boys and one for the girls. We got spring from a bed and the boys made it into an actual bed for the girls' room. When it was time to leave, the children would get up and say, "Goodbye mamma, goodbye daddy" and go home.

Even though I was somewhat shy and withdrawn like my father, I was well liked at school and was very popular. While I did not give much to the system of education, I was able to get from grade to grade though I didn't like it any better. I got passing grades by discussing the lessons with my brightest classmates. It was as if by osmosis that I absorbed the necessary minimum required to pass test. My friends also let me copy their homework. It was in the fourth grade that the chickens came home to roost. It was that year that

two things happened to me. First, I realized that there were things

taught in the fourth based upon what we learned in the third grade. I

began to see the cumulative nature of schooling and I wished that I

had studied more in the previous grades. The second thing that

happened to me was that I began to have teachers I liked. Wanting

to please the teachers was rather painful since I had rejected earlier

teachings and was limited in how much I could actually please.

I could have strangled Big Fat Geneva! After all, she started

my dislike for schooling, not to mention she was the queen of the

merry-go-round witches. But all those wasted years because of an ice

cream cone and a merry-go-round didn't make sense at all. I realized

the merry-go-round and ice cream cone were just surface

manifestations of a deeper dislike. I was really revolting against the

way people always wanted to change and control others; their values

and what they found important. In that sense I was definitely like my

father. School made me angry because it failed to take into account

my feelings and what I liked. Some people adjusted by being passive

and malleable, I have never been that way. I guess the bottom line is

that teachers do not expect children to know what is good for them or what they want, but that is not completely true. Teachers made that mistake with me because I knew the difference between how I was treated at school and how I was treated at home.

We had moved back to Fort Lauderdale from Montgomery Alabama partly because my fathers' brother and sister did not like the fact that their mother had to take care of us girls for him. Back in Fort Lauderdale, my father indulged me, perhaps even spoiled me. He was never harsh and encouraged his girls to develop their own personalities and be themselves. He was independent which made me the same way. We shared other traits like his rebelliousness, kindness and understanding. "Daddy, daddy" I said, "you didn't answer my question." My father was home from work sitting in his green comfort chair and I was immediately in his lap. He was half regaling me and half bidding Miss Betty goodbye. She stayed at our house during the day to look after me when I was forced to stay home because of my asthma. Practically every neighbor I had was like a family member and no one ever refused to come to our house to look after me if they had the time. Any and all of them would scold me or spank me and there were never any differences between them and my family because of it. Of course they never really hurt me and I didn't go home and complain. My father or mother would say "Well, if they scolded or spanked you, it must have been for a good reason. Now what did you do to deserve it?" My neighbors were an integral of my family.

"Miss Betty," said my father, "I hope Tinky was not a special burden for you today."

"Jimmy, our little Tinky is such a little lady sometimes. Do you know when her little friends come over she was like a teacher and organized the other little children? She had them all busy doing different things. When she wasn't talking or explaining something she dressed up in her mother's clothes. She stuck pillows in her cloths pretending to be grown up. She dressed up and pretended she was Miss Ora, [R.D.'s grandmother from down the street]. She even knows how to talk like a woman. No, she's no problem at all Jimmy and as a matter of fact she is pretty funny. She even mimicked Miss Ora scolding the children saying 'Now you children get out of my tomato garden ya' hear? Jimmy, she just entertains herself with whatever and whoever is around." She stopped and mused to herself then said, "It was something to behold."

"Daddy, when are you going to answer my question?" I asked, "How do you breathe underwater?"

"I'll be on my way now Jimmy, the dinner is keeping warm on the stove. You all have a nice evening now. I will watch the girls tomorrow until you get home from work. Goodnight now" said Miss Ruth leaving to return home.

"Well, I am so grateful for your being here with the girls" my father replied. "Goodnight."

"Daddy, are you going to answer my question now? I moaned. "You're a man not a fish and I thought that only fish could breathe underwater?"

"Wait Tinky, I haven't explained."

When my mother had died and my father was the only parent, he would get neighborhood women to come into the house to help us. When he got home he spent a lot of time talking to us and creating a family atmosphere. He would entertain us; we lined up and took turns being thrown in the air giggling and screaming rushing back to the line to do it again. We heard stories about his jobs from his green chair with his legs raised up on the hassock. He had placed the chair in a position where he could observe us whether

43

we were on the front porch, in the kitchen, or in the back yard.

"Well Tinky," my father began, "you're right. People don't breathe underwater like fish can. For a person to go underwater and be able to breathe he has to have a special suit. When I go underwater to fix the bottom of a ship I put on one of the suits. It keeps you dry and has a special top part that goes over your head. There are two hoses that go in the top part. One of the hoses brings in the good air that you can breathe. The other one takes out the bad air you have already breathed." He paused to peer out of the living room window.

"Daddy, will you take me to work with you?" I said. "So I can see what you look like in your fish suit? I want to draw a picture of you in your suit so you can put it in your dresser. Daddy listen to me sing like Marian Anderson!"

I began to sing with my hands folded in front of me carefully, shaping my mouth to form the exact sound of the words. My father had stopped listening as his attention was shifted to someone or something outside the wide living room window approaching the house. The storm shutter, which was lowered and latched to prevent damage to the window pane during hurricane season, was raised, giving a full view to the outside. The raised shutter was also hinged at the top which shaded the living room from the sun and prevented glare while anyone looked out of the window.

I heard the footsteps and craned my neck towards the window in time to see Jimmie-Lee and Doris escorting Miss Idella to our front door. Miss Idella was a beautician in our neighborhood. She had been married once but did not have any children. When my sisters and I had gone to have our hair done, she became our friend. My older sister Jimmie-Lee wanted to have a mother and she adopted Miss Idella as ours. Miss Idella was very sympathetic toward us. Sometimes when my father came home and we were not there, he would find us at Miss Idella's beauty parlor where we would go after school. We were fond of Miss Idella and she was fond of us too. Everybody knew her and after my mother died, she paid special attention to us girls.

Daddy rose from his chair and met them at the door.

"Jimmy I just wanted to see how you were doing with this house full of little princesses so, I came with your daughters when they told me that Tinky had to stay home because of her asthma."

Miss Idella was carrying a shopping bag which she took to the kitchen, placed on the table, and returned to the living room to speak to my father.

"I brought over a few things. Your girls and I planned a cooking project." She said.

"Jimmie-Lee will you and Juanita take the things out of the bag?" she directed her attention to my father. "The girls and I are going to make a casserole" she said.

"Miss Idella that is very thoughtful of you" said my father, "it makes me happy to know that they have someone like you to look up to and do things with them".

Miss Idella *pooh poohed* and walked to the kitchen.

My father was a very handsome man. Like I said earlier, he had a special way with people and was extremely well liked in our neighborhood and wherever we went. As I grew older I learned that women naturally liked and respected him greatly. I remember being a little jealous of other women because my father and I were so close. After my mother died, many women wanted to take care of him. Some would not hesitate to come to our house to cook, clean and to shop for the family. To us girls, Miss Idella, who we affectionately called 'Mu'Dear', was our favorite and eventually my father and Miss Idella grew to like each other. It was us who brought my father and Miss Idella together. Everyday after school we'd be at Mu'Dear's house. One day she asked if all we girls and our father could stay at her house. I don't think they ever married but Miss Idella became our step mother and my father's second "wife."

We all moved together to another big house. Mu'Dear kept the house we used to live in for her beauty business. She was a stickler for cleanliness. Everything had to be shiny, us girls could not lace anything but scrubbed. You could eat off of the bathroom floor. That's why Miss Fostina came into our lives, she was hired by Mu'Dear. She did all the washing and ironing of us girls' clothes, and Mu'Dear and Miss Fostina alternated on the cooking. During the week we ate whatever Miss Fostina or Mu'Dear cooked, but on the weekends we got to choose anything we wanted. Miss Fostina cleaned so well that there was neither dust nor dirt anywhere. I knew because Mu'Dear would sometimes punish us by making us get under the bed. That was just one of her methods; she didn't know much about children. She would ask the women who came into her beauty parlor about raising girls and she asked some of the others to make clothes for us.

Next door to the beauty parlor was a shoe shop owned by Mr. Watson. In the summer when Mr. Watson closed his shop earlier and Mu'dear was busy, we would go with Mr. Watson to the beach with his son David. We spent many summers at the beach in the surf, riding on inner tubes. We took boards and rode the waves in. We all enjoyed the water and the sand too because of the beautiful shapes that were able to be created. Down the street from our house was a drug store. The store had a lot of nice gifts in it; I used to save my money and buy gifts for Mu'Dear and daddy. One Christmas, I bought Mu'Dear a waffle iron and another time, I bought her a beautiful Cinderella clock. I got to be such a good customer that Mr. Walter started letting me put things on lay-away, taking a quarter or fifty cents at a time.

Chapter Four: My Step Mother

I spent the other half of my short childhood with Mu'Dear. She was a business woman and had gone back to school to get her high school diploma. She later went on to Florida A&M University and became a teacher. She talked to us and the young people in the neighborhood encouraging us to do well in school and continue our education. Mu'Dear made more money than my father but my father was the stability in our lives, Mu'Dear traveled a lot. She was a strong woman, independent and self motivated; the kind my father liked. They got along very well.

MuDear's whole family was progressive. It was a tradition in her family to excel, to be in business, be a community leader, and to help the less fortunate. Some of them lived in Clewiston Florida where I became their favorite niece. She also had family in Lake City Florida, A sister-in-law a brother and their children. We used to go there for family reunions. It was a whole different lifestyle than Fort Lauderdale's. They lived in a town that had no stores. For entertainment we took long walks along the countryside. Everything we ate was raised on the farm and my cousins were used to milking cows, feeding chickens and slopping pigs. They saw livestock slaughtered in the morning, dressed in the afternoon, and cooked on the table for dinner. They grew, tended, picked, and canned fruits and vegetables. They also drank spring water pumped from a well.

On the farm we had big breakfasts: eggs, hot biscuits, bacon, sausages, and grits. After breakfast we would watch as my uncle killed animals and cured meats. He taught us to Barbecue, pick walnuts, string beans, and collard greens for dinner. It was so much fun. My cousins always saw us as superior to them because we were from the city. I guess they thought that we had all the refinements of life. Where they lived, life was close to the Earth and in the warmer months they went barefoot. Some of them left the farm to come to Fort Lauderdale for school becoming some of the best students in the school. I always thought that they excelled in school as a way of making up for their country origins, which they felt were inferior to our city backgrounds. Once they got off of the farm they continued to do well in school, went on to college, and entered different professions.

Mu'Dear's father lived in Fort Lauderdale. He was Aunt Della's brother, known as Grand Daddy Allen. He was a very strong man who usually spoke few words. We would sit together and he would feed me when I used to go visit him. He would talk to me and smile as he answered many of my questions. Sometimes we would say "nunya," as in none of your business. This was his answer to some of the questions I asked and if I asked why, he would say, "you have no business asking and you don't have to know."

Mu'Dear came into my life bringing some of the most meaningful and wonderful experiences. I was adopted as a favorite niece by Mu'Dear's Aunt Della. I was like the daughter she never had. I looked forward to the end of school which I continued to hate. I was about nine years old when I started going to Aunt Della's. The trips to Clewiston and to Aunt Della were over many roads that were unpaved at the time. The three hour trip was somewhat in the interior of Florida and past the swamps and the Everglades. To a child it was a somewhat tiresome ride but well tolerated knowing that Aunt Della and more of her family were waiting for me.

Aunt Della was special in her town; Mrs. Della Tobias. In those days there was limited education and opportunity so those who managed to rise above the rest did what they could for others. She did work for the people and churches. She had a store in which she would extend credit and keep a book of notes and accounts for all those she knew to be trustworthy and in need. She owned a restaurant with Uncle Henry, a very large man who always wore suspenders and was very jolly.

At a big white house trimmed in green lived Mr. Sleepy, Aunt Della's chauffeur. The Rooming house had plenty of people living upstairs and downstairs, my cousin George owned the theatre. Aunt Della slept in one room and Uncle Henry slept in another. I had my own room down the hall across from the living room complete with my own oil lamp. I always kept it on very low in my room so that I could see everything. Also, if Aunt Della wanted me, I could go quickly. Later on, when Aunt Della became ill, she taught me how to fill the lamp with kerosene and light it. After Aunt Della became sick, I always kept my lamp filled just in case.

Aunt Della helped build the church in the black neighborhood. When I would go to Sunday school, I was always called on to sing. They all knew I was Mrs. Tobias's niece visiting from the city. Knowing I would be called on to sing at church, some of my friends and I would gather in Aunt Della's veranda and practice because of the piano in there. The children and I loved to play on it. My friend Murial was really good at playing the piano. She had taken lessons from her aunt who played very well.

When I got to Clewiston, all the children treated me like royalty because I was Aunt Della's niece. I was revered and sometimes I took them to her restaurant. Other times after we finished practicing for Sunday school, I took the neighborhood kids to Aunt Della's store and let them pick out something they wanted. When it was time for me to return to Fort Lauderdale, I was in Aunt Della's big car—a blue dodge, one of the few new cars around. As we drove through the neighborhood on the way to the bus depot, all the children would follow alongside the car in the billowing dust; inside I would be waving goodbye to them, anxious to visit Aunt Della again.

The next summer, I breathlessly awaited my return to

Clewiston. I was looking forward to a whole new adventure with

Aunt Della. On the way I thought about the ways in which I would

help her and the bedtime stories that I would tell. The joy was at its

pinnacle within me the instant my bus had pulled into the Clewiston

Florida station where I was met by the chauffeur Mr. Sleepy. Mr.

Sleepy had eyes that were just about closed all the time and his

greeting of me was nothing short of royal. I felt as if he efficiently

retrieved my bag from the side of the bus and effortlessly stowed it in

the trunk of the limousine. He teased me for not having the usual

child traveler tag my daddy and Mu'Dear insisted on me wearing, as I

had done in the previous summers.

The familiar bus drive from home to Aunt Della's brought

with it rush of fond memories. The children in the neighborhood

knew Aunt Della's big blue dodge and she must have hinted that I

was arriving. As soon as we turned into the dusty road they spotted

us ad walked alongside the car. I waved to them feeling like a

celebrity as we stopped in front of Aunt Della's house. When I got

out of the car, I promised to return to the neighborhood kids as soon as I attended to whatever Aunt Della had in mind for my first day in Clewiston.

That was the beginning. The whole summer I entertained Aunt Della. I read the bible, cooked for her without using salt, and we practiced our prayers together. I also practiced my singing with her. Aunt Della had low blood pressure. When she came home from working in the store or at the café I used to rub her arms and rub caster oil into her scalp because she was going bald. We always thought the treatment would grow hair but it never did. A very short woman about 3'2", Aunt Della and I literally saw eye to eye. Unconsciously I saw her as a mate because she was extremely short. She was in a class by herself. I really enjoyed being with her and she enjoyed my company just as much.

I thought how Mu'Dear's family was different from my father's. My father's family took life as it came and tried to make the most of it while Mu'Dear's family made life what they wanted it to be. They were leaders in all areas of their community; Aunt Della's husband Uncle Henry was enterprising as well. He serviced the local sugar mill workers with lunch complete with soda and sandwiches, and articles of clothing. From his wagon, Uncle Henry sold vegetables. He also boiled and parched peanuts, which he sold by the bag. Aunt Della was the epitome of a business woman. She had three grown sons but no little ones and greatly enjoyed having me with her. She liked to hear me say prayers and sing like Marian Anderson. Aunt Della was well dressed and groomed; all of her clothes were custom made. She was esteemed and people relied upon her. I liked being among my aunt and uncle knowing how important they were to their community. It made me feel uplifted and needed as well. My need for this esteem stayed with me and motivated me for a long time. Yes, now that I think of it, I am sure my stays' at Aunt Della's was the origin of such needs.

I enjoyed having the ability to provide small treats for the children, who were truly happy with ice cream, candy, soda pop, popsicles, and cookies. By doing this, I realized how Mu'Dear's personal joy derived from encouraging others, and how Aunt Della's sense of accomplishment originated from assisting others in her community. From the time that Mu'Dear and her family came into my life I felt more goodwill towards others. I knew that I would not be as rebellious in school and this new feeling of kindness brought with it forgiveness for my first grade teacher Big Fat Geneva, the queen of the merry-go-round witches.

Playing with the neighborhood kids and working in Aunt Della's store went by like a blur. I was eleven years old visiting Aunt Della one summer when she fell ill. She was forced to stop working in the store and the café. That summer, I spent most of my time back and forth with her to the doctor's office. I wanted Aunt Della to get better, she was extremely important to me, and a close friend. Aunt Della would always listen to me and she would laugh at the bed time stories I used to tell her. She said that she never heard stories like them and I explained that it was because I made them up, which she thought was very clever. The whole time that Aunt Della was ill, I cooked for her and served her in bed. I wouldn't let her do anything when she did not feel like getting up and moving about. That summer was the last summer that I spent with Aunt Della. Since she was sick, it was difficult for her to watch me. She suggested that I visit over the Easter and Christmas vacations.

During those short eight weeks, Aunt Della's illness must have changed me somehow. On the bus, my state of mind was laid to rest by the hypnotic drone of the engine. I streaked home, southward bound along the flat peninsula and east toward the

Atlantic shore of Clewiston to Fort Lauderdale. I saw the swamps, the Everglades, and the usual sights in reverse. Somehow I could tell that this trip was unlike any other. It seemed that while my eyes were focused on the shapes and colors outside of the window, what I was really seeing was my own life. It was a very different kind of experience; I never knew that people could have such thoughts about themselves. Aunt Della's brought some kind of transformation though unnoticed, unbidden, and unexpected until now. I wondered if I still wanted to organize the neighborhood children to play "school" acting as the teacher giving them schoolwork to do. How much I had grown in such a short period.

To be honest, I don't think I was ever much of a child. People used to talk about how lady like I was even as a youngster. They kidded my father about my grownup social grace and command of the neighborhood children. When I was singing Marian Anderson, they marveled at how I stood poised, even at eight years old. I loved the "Five Blind Boys" and went to hear them at churches. I loved Sam Cook's singing and I listened to his records a lot. I would listen to Marian Anderson recordings and practice sounding like her—A Capella.

I took voice lessons and piano lessons with Mrs. Lovett every Saturday for two years. I developed a rich vibrato and could hold the notes for a long time, practicing my singing in church. I always liked to hear the congregation say, "Amen" and "Alleluia" after my singing. My parents were always very proud of me. I knew many of the Negro spirituals and some I knew by heart. In front of the congregation I could hear myself dragging out the notes, "Leeeeeead me, guiiiiiiiiide me, alooooooooooonnng the waaaay, fooooooor if yooouu leeeeeead meeeeeee, I caannnnnnnnot straaaaaaay." One of my other favorites was, "I think that I shall never see a poem as lovely as a tree." I loved church, especially the feeling of God's presence that the church contained. B.Y.P.U. was one of my favorite organizations. The church's religious summer camps were very nice and increased my interest in church and God. I was our church's representative at bible school, youth conferences and conventions. At school I took drum lessons and practiced with recordings of Cannon Ball Adderly.

At school, I was on the cheerleading squad and I was attending many of the schools events. My extracurricular activities however, were replacing my time for studying. I was still scarred from earlier in my academic career, and I guess I was just being contrary. In any event I spent very little if any time at all studying. I thought to myself, "is this a childish phase?" Would it pass now that I felt older?

I hadn't had an asthma attack in a while. People always said that I would grow out of it. I remember how there were always suggestions from my neighbors about how I could fight asthma.

"Never go barefoot" said one of my neighbors. Another neighbor of mine suggested the tines of a fork could cure asthma. I remember slamming the kitchen door twisting the fork tines into the shape of a cross. As I went to pick it up, my mother ran to me and told me not to touch it and not ever to touch it. These were things that were done to protect the house and the children, like putting garlic around our necks. It was awful but we, as children, just accepted it. I never did find out what had to be done with the fork or why it couldn't be touched. The fork was green, a different color from the other forks, whatever that meant. Anyway I was shedding asthma without the folk cures. Did that mean I was growing up? Surely the fact I had not had an attack meant it was true. No more wheezing, no more watery eyes, no more death defying gasps for precious air. There were no more middle of the night emergencies, broken rest and frightened, worried parents. Was I grown up now? Was I somehow, different?

When the asthma finally ceased for good I discovered a lot about the world, especially about the outdoors and Jimmy-Lee. She taught me how to ride a bike and we went places together. We even rode our bikes to school together. Jimmy-Lee became my protector. When we rode our bikes she made sure that I always rode farthest from traffic. She kept an eye on me to see if I was tiring, she wouldn't joyride ahead of me and wait, she would always be close by. Jimmy-Lee always made sure all my books and lunch were safely stored away on the bike, and that my money was always in a secure place. There were times in school she would leave her class and come to mine to check on me. Jimmy-Lee eventually became the big sister whom every little sister dreams of. She took me places and coming home without me was out of the question. On top of that, Jimmie-Lee kept all of my secrets; she was the domestic kind of girl, almost motherly. I was the opposite of Jimmy-Lee, a risk taker, but Jimmy-Lee and I only became closer.

It wasn't that I broke the rules, bent them or ignored them; I did things for which rules did not exist but, not in a way that was worrisome. I just wanted a little more freedom. As I got older, having fun was slipping out the bedroom window to see my friends or escaping a beating from Mu'Dear. Mu'Dear would not spank you at the time of the wrongdoing. The small offenses would culminate as one beating. "It's in the bag" Mu'Dear would say, meaning that she was logging the small infractions. Sometimes when I knew I had a lot in the bag and I did something wrong, I would take off running on general principal.

Being allowed outside was still relatively new to me. Jimmy-Lee helped me make the transition without complaining or preaching, she wanted to make up for the years lost to my being kept indoors. Jimmy-Lee could be depended upon to let me back in through the window when I snuck outside. My instructions to her were very clear: before she was to do anything else, she was to tiptoe a little ways down the hall to make sure my father was asleep. If she could not see him sleeping, she was to listen for the sound of a car engine trying to start followed by the sound of a chimpanzee scolding no one in particular. If these sounds were heard, daddy was sound asleep. In the event that she was caught looking into his room, she was to make up some story about sleepwalking and return to our room. If daddy was asleep, Jimmy-Lee was to return immediately, take the feather I kept on my dresser for such occasions, and twirl it lightly in Doris' nostril. If Doris did not jump up wide-eyed and spastic, she was asleep. If she were pretending to sleep in order to catch me sneaking out, Jimmy-Lee was to tell Doris I had a picture of her dipping a cup into the rice pudding Mu'Dear made for the Beauticians Ball. Mu'Dear saw the missing rice pudding, heard us all deny it and promised stiff penance for the liar. If Doris argued, Jimmy-Lee was to remind her of the picture I had of her at the school dance, all wrapped up and in love. It was a long shot because it depended on Doris forgetting I got my camera two days after the rice pudding was missing; I had to take the risk.

Sometimes, I was caught doing things and would have to face Mu'Dear. When I was older, she used to whip me with the cord of the iron but, I rebelled against whipping so much that she tried something new. Standing on one leg for an hour in the bathroom was Mu'Dear's new brand of correction, a punishment guaranteed to bring in line even the most wayward child without laying a hand on them. I was on punishment one day when Doris came in. "Hi, Doris!" I said cheerfully with one leg raised and arms extended outwards for poise and balance. With my chin raised, I looked heroically into the vast audience that filled the stadium. I was the center of an Olympic event where I would astonish the world with excellence in one leg standing. I was determined the Americans would win the gold in this event concentrating hard not to fall, wobble, or waver. The world would know the truth; in this event I was in a league of my own.

"I think I'll tell Mu'Dear you're in here having fun."

"Please Doris, the judges are watching me. Anyway, tell…tell! See if I care. Nobody believes a snitch anyway. Mu'Dear is a mean woman!" I said angrily, more at Doris for taking away my perfect concentration than at Mu'Dear.

"Ooooooh I'm telling!" said Doris shocked, wide-eyed and impressed by my brazenness.

"Go tell her *that* you little snitch. See what you get. Do you think you are going to get a piece of Miss Ora's sweet potato pie? Or, maybe you think you are going to get a diamond ring? A fur coat? No, I'm serious, go tell you little snitch and come back here and show me what you got for telling on me."

"Please Doris," I pleaded mockingly, "Would you do that for me little snitch?" Doris sniffed and left the bathroom.

"Don't forget now sweetie," I shouted at her back, remember what nice photographs I take!"

Just as I began counting as high as I could before losing my balance, my father appeared at the door.

My father was my pal during punishment. He would make a pretense about having to use the bathroom which meant of course that I had to leave. Well, that was rest time. I could go to the kitchen and take a load off. My father was something of an actor. "Delois!" he'd say in a shout so all could hear his stern voice, "Come out while I use the bathroom and be sure to come back in when I leave." Meanwhile, he would find some reason to stay in the bathroom for a long time.

Since I was growing up, I had the feeling I would miss going to the hospital. The hospital that I went to when I was younger was very small, no larger than the clinic my god-father and god-uncle made for our neighborhood. I was taken to the hospital when I was younger because the asthma attacks where so severe that it was thought that I wouldn't survive. The reasoning behind my hospital stays was that it was better to be on the safe side. I was getting familiar with the movements and behavior of doctors and nurses. I grew accustomed to sitting quietly outside of the emergency room being observed, treated, or being told that the attack was over and I could go home. There were other times when I spent several nights at the hospital. I was the center of attention and I was usually happy there. People did everything I told them to do. All I had to do was say, "bring me a teddy bear" or "bring me a necklace." "Bring me a, ah, ah, a puzzle!" "Can I have a bracelet? A ring?" the sky was the limit. "Bring me a piece of Miss Ora's sweet potato pie," and whatever I asked for would appear with the next person's visit.

Hospitals are small and very personal and I had grown to like them because of those characteristics. I occasionally enjoyed the change of routine which gave me a chance to observe people, talk, and pretend. My doctor would walk into my room and I would start.

"I'm Doctor Shuska," I said. "Did you take your medicine little boy?" My doctor was patient enough to play along. "Now little boy, you sit here and stick out your tongue," he did so. "Now, I want you to eat all of your vegetables so that you can get better."

Doctor Shuska continued to play along. "Okay Doctor Shuska, tell me how do *you* feel today? Does the doctor feel better? Are you breathing easier?"

To me, hospitals had a kind of grace. People were being helped. I was impressed with the doctors and nurses, they inspired trust. They gracefully accepted the dependency people imposed upon them. I liked that, even at thirteen years old, I knew that I wanted to be like that; professional, efficient, and esteemed. In fact, I enjoyed hospitals so much that in high school I worked in one. I loved it.

Since my god-father and his brother owned the small private hospitals, I had plenty of influences that attracted me to the medical field. I had a chance to go from patient to patient, showing them how understanding we were at the hospital and how they didn't have to worry. "Can I pour you some water? Can I fluff your pillow? What about a magazine? Sure, you can lean on me while I walk you to the sun room." I liked comforting the patients, we even prayed together. At fourteen I helped to deliver a baby. An expectant mother entered the hospital and the doctor was not around. She was in a lot of pain and I told her I would help. I gave her a prep first.

Following my past training in such things, I escorted the screaming woman to a room while the nurses got the delivery room ready.

I stood by the mother in the bed until it was time to go into the delivery room. Before the delivery room was available, the baby's head came out. I told the mother to push. The doctors and nurses arrived came into the hall midway to the delivery room and the baby was delivered. The doctor cut the umbilical cord and held him upside down; I was visibly shaken from all of the blood and let out a "Ewwwwww!" The doctor explained to me that the inside of the human body is cleaner than the human mouth. The baby started to cry right away and all I could do was laugh. I watched as they cleansed the child removing the mucus and blood before I took it to the nursery. As I looked at it, I imagined it was my own child.

Another experience I had in the hospital was with a man who was having a seizure. I knew from my previous training to place something in his mouth to prevent choking. I learned a lot from being around my god-father. I learned how about sterilization, scrubbing, filling out paper work, and other office information. Dr. Moorhead's thought that I would become a doctor.

I was like my father, kind and gentle, I was like Mu'Dear professional and efficient, and I was like Aunt Della, capable of helping the misfortunate. The qualities I acquired from my relatives helped shape my personality. My father was a healer of sorts. It was he who would tell me how beautiful and precious I was to him after some of my classmates at school called me ugly. If you didn't know him personally you could mistake him for a diplomat, an ambassador, or statesman. I must say he carried a certain innate dignity and class into all social situations. But, he also shunned school and I often imagine that it was for the same reason that I did. That is why I am glad Mu'Dear went through school and beyond to counter my father's influence on my academic career. She was able to balance his effects and forced me to put my life in perspective. If I wanted to be successful I would have to have an education and with Mu'Dear's perseverance that would certainly serve as my inspiration.

Chapter Five: Contact with Catholicism

One year a woman came to my school and sang "Getting to know you, getting to know all about you…" She was a white missionary. Her manner and purpose impressed me. You can imagine how her singing impressed me, I started thinking that I could go on a mission, sing like Marian Anderson and serve God too. When I was in high school, I had to do an essay on religion but, I needed someone to do the paper with. A boy named Oliver, who liked me a lot, was doing his essay on Catholicism and said I could join him. Assisting in the writing of that paper had a lasting impression upon me.

Eventually, I wanted to know more about Catholicism. I went to Oliver's church, Our Lady of Annunciation, where I met the monsignor O'Hare. I asked why people were not instructed to confess their sins directly to God. Why did the priests listen to confessions when they were not God himself? Father O'Hare gave an explanation of it and invited me to come to mass with Oliver. I liked the singing but the majestic rituals and the somberness of the ringing of the chalice was overwhelming. I loved the priest's robes and his princely bearing. I always thought of myself in terms of royalty and felt quite at home with all the ritual and elaborateness of the catholic ceremonies.

"Dee-Lois," Father O'Malley said.

I did not flinch or tense up. I simply thought about how the years of hearing my name mispronounced might soon end. As father spoke, two things were on my mind. I was thinking that what I was contemplating would mean a change of my name. I would make sure the new name would be one that no one would mispronounce; a blessed respite. I had started a list of possible new names I liked and Noelita was still my favorite. That is, if it was available at the place and time my new name was confirmed. My name is spelled D-e-l-o-i-s, pronounced like the French "Del-Wa." But, since I was about seven, I became aware of everyone's mispronunciation of it.

Fortunately, the awesome beauty of the priests' study did not leave much time for me to continue my thoughts about how even the priests mispronounced my name.

The Father's study was the beauty that I had come to expect from the Catholic Church; the carved wall paneling, the bas relief depicting historical and divine scenery, the antiques and tapestries. The ringing of the chalice was so solemn and beautiful it often brought tears to my eyes. The awesome beautiful cathedral with statues was what attracted me to the Catholic Church. The priest was not aware of the deference I had for his beautiful flowing robes with their royal braid and embroidery. When I focused my attention back on Father O'Malley he was saying:

"Young Miss Blakely, known to us as Dee-Lois, I have been the Shepard of this flock here at Saint Ann's parish for years." Not once during that time has a 14 year old black or white, come forth to announce that she hears the calling to serve God. This is all quite novel to us here but our position is to believe everything that you say. If you say you are called by God to serve, who are we to doubt it? God indeed calls people. That is one reason why Dee-Lois, we have accommodated your request of this church."

I forgave him for mispronouncing my name again.

"As you've noticed we have sped up the confirmation processes for you. One thing I know for sure. If ever there is a young lady who is always and absolutely positive about everything she does or perceives it's our Miss Dee-Lois Blakely. Count it as a gift that in all things you have a positive spirit. The church recognizes you are a bit cheeky and we shall be in prayer for you about that, but mostly we appreciate your bright inquiring mind. We must pray however, that with all your talents and your cheek, you will in fact, do something benefiting someone else; even if by accident. We also believe that in helping others God might overlook your rather thick skin. For you not to serve God would be futile. It would mean a superficial life like some others who thought they had a calling but were merely looking for a hiding place from worldly situations."

Father O'Malley sat back in his velvet chair and regarded me as he continued to smile having finished his speech. I understood the first half of what he said but I didn't know what the second part was about unless he was trying to challenge me. I felt he had been a bit critical. Maybe one day I will understand everything he said. What does *futile* mean anyway?

My smile never left my face. I stood up, curtsied and thank Father O'Malley for no doubt was his words of encouragement and wisdom. Rather than prolong the visit I exited as quickly as I had come. All this was started by riding in Aunt Della's big car and having all the neighborhood children revere me. I thought I was a princess, it was regal. The ritual in the Baptist Church was not as sophisticated and so it lost me. You could tell the priest anything you wanted, no matter what I said he would smile and continue our conversation. Soon, the priest gave me a set of rosaries and showed me how to say the rosaries. Oliver was an alter boy and told me all the duties of one. I began to study catechism, I told my father about it. At that time, Mu'Dear was going to Florida A&M to get her first degree. I started catechism class twice a week and Oliver would go with me. After I graduated from catechism class, they gave me my baptism and catholic godparents, Roy and Grace Mizells. They owned the Mizell funeral home and were both morticians.

I was baptized on Saturday and confirmed on the following day, this was going to be the second time. The first was at the age of twelve in Mount Olive Baptist Church, my first love before meeting

Oliver. My step mother was a Baptist and encouraged us to go to

church. My father was never really interested in going to church, he

did not believe in it. To him, the most important thing was the way

that you lived your life from day to day and the way you treated

others. That was his religion. Although my father was not against

going to church, he did not think of it much as a practice. Religious

activity in the family before I ventured into Catholicism was just as

conventional as it would have been in any other family. I went to

Sunday's services regularly, participated in church activities, was a

member in the church choir, and actively involved in Sunday school

among many other responsibilities. It was nothing out of the

ordinary; we were all devotees except for my father who always came

on special occasions to sing or read verses from the Bible.

Now, I was a Catholic and Sister Laura was who I wanted to

be like. I had come in contact with her when I began frequenting the

Catholic Church. She was very friendly, tolerating and

understanding. I pestered her a lot with questions, and without

showing any signs of exasperation, she would answer all of my

questions. The more she answered my questions the more curious I became. I ended up liking her and her ways and I imagined myself being her. I didn't want to be white but I wanted to love and serve God the way Sister Laura did. I wanted to go to a convent. I used to spend time with Sister Laura eating in the convent and talking about becoming a nun. She told me that I couldn't become a nun because I was too young. I told her I still was going to become a nun and she wrote a letter about me to an order in the Bahamas. The letter from them said I was too young. I was told that it was okay because I really wanted to enter the order she came from, somewhere up north. Actually, any convent that would prepare me to serve the world was sufficient. Serving it was my realistic goal but serving the world was my ideal and my passion.

Chapter Six: The Night Before

The night before I left was an extremely exciting night, I did not sleep at all. It is a night I shall remember for as long as I live. It seemed that the gentle morning light of dawn would never peak through the endless, sleepless night. All of my neighbors, classmates, childhood friends—virtually the whole community had come to say goodbye. This would be the last time most of them would ever see me. They came, sat, looked, and waited with me for the moment when I would depart and no longer call this familiar place home. The party started off somewhat like a wake. Most people just sat and waited as if they were expecting something from me. I don't know if that something was a goodbye speech or a eulogy for the life I was leaving behind.

I'll always remember my baby sister Juanita Jackie actually sniggled at me. I couldn't keep Doris out of my bedroom where she kept peeping at my trunk. While Jimmy-Lee welcomed the visitors and made sure they were comfortable, Delois would be leaving in a little while.

"I guess you all know she is going to New York City to become a nun?" Jimmy-Lee reminded the guest. "Yes—she will be out in a little while" stated Jackie.

Yes, I remember my father kept smiling and asking, "Baby, are you alright?" I was fine. You'd be fine too if practically the whole colored part of town was in your house to give you a send off to New York City. I was very happy if just a tad sleepy. I was having a good time being the center of attention. I knew that if I changed my mind and decided not to go I could. These were my decisions and I felt quite good about them. This was all my doing, this was my own thing! I knew that I would almost kiss the train that would carry me to New York City.

I remember Mu'Dear well that night. I remember she planned and prepared for the evening and for my leaving. She had orchestrated the entire send off with my Aunt Ruth, who lived right next door. I remember how the two of them huddled together, comforting and supporting each other through this emotional event. I surprised everyone by dressing up. I figured this was the time to show off for the last time and at the same time, give them an idea about what their first nun from the neighborhood was going to look like in her clothes. Doris was curious about the big trunk she was still peeping into the room so I asked her to come and help me dress. When I told her I was going to dress like a nun all she could do was laugh; her way of relieving the nervous tension that had overcame her. We closed the bedroom door. "How would Delois look as a nun?" We both thought. That was the question we were going to answer. All those present would have their curiosity satisfied and I could share to a greater degree my coming experience.

Doris and I began taking things out of the trunk. I had been given a list of articles that I had to bring with me to the convent. At sixteen, a girl knows nothing about buying the clothes that nuns wear. A local priest Alex, and Sister Laura, helped me find and purchase some of the specialized things needed by nuns. Earlier that day, the trunk had been filled with an assortment of unfamiliar shapes of fabric in black and white. The list I was given contained a lot of different items like these "special shoes," not just conservative black shoes but old fashioned shoes—the kind that old people wear. These were the first thing Doris laughed at. Next were the stockings; thick, black, and cotton. The slip I had to have was long and black as well. Doris had another good laugh. Next, we took out a long black skirt, "the kind the, holy and sanctified women wear!" Doris cheerfully pointed out.

The blouse had long sleeves with a high collar and buttons. Doris commented that everything was long and black. She also observed that every part of me would be covered up. Then, we pulled out something and we couldn't tell what it was. We kept playing with it and trying it in different positions until we figured out what we had to do with it. It turned out to be a cape which fitted on the blouse. Next we confronted a long thin scarf which was as you guessed it, black. We decided we would figure it out if we kept it in mind that the final look should be "nun like." So, with that morphological goal, we created an image in our minds of what would be a reasonable nun to show the waiting guest.

I began to dress with Doris's help. There were other items in the trunk, but we became aware of the waiting guest in the living room and decided to construct my nun attire from among the items already identified. When I had dressed, the other unidentified items in the trunk fell into place. Soon there was nothing left in the trunk to figure out. It was now time for me to share my costume with those waiting for me in the living room.

Doris was to leave the room ahead of me. We opened the door a crack to see our audience. We tried not to make a sound. They saw Doris giggling as she entered the living room. Quickly, I closed the door so they could not see what Doris had been giggling at. I wanted to make a grand entrance so I thought best to forget Doris's prelude. A giggle was not an appropriate prelude to my grand entrance. When I thought no one was looking at the door, I stepped into the living room. Everyone stopped what they were doing, or saying; perhaps even thinking. All eyes were on me. It was a solemn occasion…too solemn. I thought we were at a wake or a funeral. It was as if someone had died. I had to do something quick to restore some kind of merriment. I wanted to cheer them up. My long garments fanned out around me in a blur of black and white circles.

John broke the ice by asking some silly questions. He was always clowning around and laughing at his own jokes. But his questions got people to relax again. Later on that night, John asked me why I didn't want to get married. I told him that it was because I didn't want a family. I explained as best I could that I wanted another kind of life. John was clearly puzzled. He was very fond of me and he thought that I did not like him. I told him that I did like him but that I <u>loved</u> God and I wanted to serve Him until I died. Throughout the night I repeated the same thing to anyone who asked about my decision. I said that I wanted to sing and dance in my nun clothes and when the music started, that I did. Everyone laughed, this was the Delois everyone knew and loved.

There were many questions put forth to the future nun, they called it, "going to the nunnery." I explained that I would have a lot to tell them about the experience when I returned to visit. The night continued with a dinner spread, dancing and merriment. As the evening wore on, some of my friends and neighbors began hugging me and saying, "Goodbye." I wondered if becoming a nun meant living a cloistered existence without seeing family and friends ever again; going to live with God forever. It was with these onerous thoughts that I said goodbye to my friends and the town of Fort Lauderdale Florida. People arrived as others left the party. I felt I was constantly saying hello or goodbye. I also felt these people would be going with me in a very special way. Even though they did not understand what I was doing they seemed happy for me. They were happy I made a choice as to what I wanted to do with my life. I overheard some of the adults speaking with my parents. They all agreed that what I was doing was a good thing. "If she wants to go and serve God, let her go and serve him" I heard them say.

The house began to empty and my younger sisters went to bed. A few close friends stayed with me through the wee hours and saw the dawning with me. We reminisced about our good times at school, in the neighborhood, at the beach, at football games and dances. We talked about how we would miss each other and doing things together. The sun was completely out and shining, my friends and I ate breakfast. I excused myself and disappeared into the bathroom. I bathed and groomed myself. My girl friends who remained, Jimmy-Lee, and Mu'Dear fussed over me. They helped me dress and reminded me of things I might have forgotten: how to behave on the train, where to keep my money, my food and so forth. They instructed me on what to eat first and how to repack the lunchbox after each meal. They gave me hints on how to make the food last longer and how to stretch my money.

From another room, Juanita noticed I was only taking the new clothes kept asking me about the things I was leaving behind. "Do you want this?" she would ask about articles of clothing or other possessions of mine. I told her that she could keep most of the things that I was leaving. Now Juanita was wide awake. Realizing how long I would be away, she started asking if I had to go and if I would be coming back.

"Yes, Juanita I have to go and no, I am not coming back" I said.

"Why aren't you coming back Delois?" said Juanita tearfully.

"I am giving my life to God," I explained.

"Why are you giving your life to God?"

"Well, because I love God…I love God a lot."

Chapter Seven: Trip to the Convent

My train was scheduled to leave at 7:30 A.M. We loaded three cars of well-wishers to accompany me to the train station. When the front door to my house was slammed shut behind me, I began to say goodbye to our house, my aunt's house next door, the street where I lived, the neighborhood and the town. The town had been good to me. As we approached the train station my mind was no longer on my past. My excitement grew so much at the sight of the train. I thought surely I would leap out of the car and dash to board the train, forgetting to embrace those who so graciously came to say goodbye.

My father could not stop the car fast enough; I could not wait to get to New York City! We all got out of the car and everyone moved to grab something. I was not allowed to carry anything onto the train. They all wanted to board the train with me and escort me to my seat to make sure everything was safely stowed or conveniently placed near me. My father was the last person with me on the train these final minutes. He told me that if I wanted to return home, at any time, I could. If I got tired of being a nun, I was welcome back home. He hugged me and never said goodbye then walked away as the conductor shouted, "All aboard!" My father turned around to look at me before he left the car I was to ride in. All my well-wishers were now stationed under my window readying to wave their last goodbyes as the train lurched forward to an imperceptible crawl.

The train moved very, very slowly. This was the first time I traveled anywhere without my family on my own to a place I had never seen before. I remembered that everybody in the south went north; I thought of the Underground Railroad. I knew nothing about what the north was like. It seemed people from my town liked going north. Everything I was familiar with quickly flashed before my eyes now as the train picked up speed. Soon the city skyline, the last familiar site, was in the distance. Now I could no longer recognize the landscape or buildings. I was outside of Fort Lauderdale, slipping in and out of small towns with names I had never heard of before.

Places I had not seen before became part of my new world experience. As I began to see more new places and faces of strangers, I began to cry. I missed my family and neighborhood; working at the hospital as a candy striper; the old people I went to the store for; my bicycle; my close friends John, Lucille, Veronica, Gwendolyn, Vargie and Benji. I missed the safe and familiar life I had taken for granted.

I cried loud enough for a stranger to come ask me what was wrong. I told him that I wanted to go home. He asked where I was going and I told him that I was entering a convent. The stranger laughed; he said that he thought that was the funniest thing he ever heard. He thought I was making the whole thing up; I was, according to him, "inventing fairy tales." I did not share any more with him and instead, I told him I was going to visit a friend in New York City. After that I left to go to the bathroom. While in the bathroom I remembered what my mother had told me about not telling strangers all of my business. To avoid further conversation with that man, I politely sat elsewhere when I got out of the bathroom.

"JACKSONVILLE FLORIDA!" was the sound that awakened me. The conductor announced our arrival for all to hear and to awaken sleeping passengers who wanted to detrain. I jumped straight up. I told the porter I was going to New York City and asked if I had to change trains. He explained that this was a rest stop. I could get off of the train if I wanted to. As the train stopped, I got off to call home. First I spoke to daddy and Mu'Dear. They asked me where I was and if I wanted to return home. I told them that I didn't want to return home and that I was still going to the convent. I felt happy at the thought of accomplishing the goal I set out to do.

"I miss you…and I love you so much Tinky" said my father.

"I miss you and I love you and Mu'dear so much too" I said, trying to keep my voice steady.

They wished me well and we said goodbye again. I returned to the train and from that time on, my mind was not on the towns that slipped by, or the states we passed through. My mind was on arriving in New York City. Once in a while a strange face would smile warmly and I would reciprocate, but not for too long, I didn't want those strangers getting any ideas. The porters on the train became my friends. They told me where to get food on the train and things like our arrival time and the number of stops left. Some of them, noticing I had been on the train since the original station, asked me about myself. I explained I was going to a convent to be a nun. One of the porters said that he was happy for me. He thought what I was doing was a good thing by giving my life to God. I then told him about Sister Laura. He then told me that he had never seen a black nun before.

It seemed like I had been riding for a week when we arrived at a place called Newark New Jersey. I got excited because I had a friend who lived in Monmouth New Jersey. I asked the porters how far Monmouth was from Newark and how far it was from New York City. One of the porters informed me that the train did not go directly to Monmouth and that I had to get off the train and take a bus. My friend, Horace, lived on a military base and I was going to visit him before continuing to New York City. I got off of the train with the porters' help; I had my trunk and other luggage to think about. The porter said that I could leave my trunk on the train and pick it up at Pennsylvania Station in New York City.

I got off the train in Newark in search of my friend in Monmouth, New Jersey. While standing on the platform at the station, I saw and escalator. I wanted to know where it led, but I was afraid to get on it since I had never seen one before. Someone told me that I had to ride the escalator up in order to get to the street and the buses. I asked the kind man if he would help me up with my bag, I was scared to ride the escalator alone. He did, I thanked him and searched for the bus that would take me to Monmouth.

I boarded the bus that would take me to Monmouth and got off the bus at the military base then approached the gate. I informed the guard there who I wanted to see. The guard called Horace and told me where to go to wait for him. Horace had lived in my neighborhood in Fort Lauderdale, we grew up together. We met in the designated place and Horace told me that he wanted to escort me to New York City so that I wouldn't have to be alone. As we talked I told him about my ride from Florida. I told him that I missed my family. Horace said that he would really like to show me New York City before I signed in at the convent; he was like a big brother to me. I stayed on the base until Horace finished his work day. I slept until he was ready to take me to New York City.

Upon our arrival in the fast city, Horace took me to his Aunt Mae's house on Bedford Street in Brooklyn. I stayed there until the weekend when Horace was able to join me at his aunt's home. I had a ball with Horace. We went to Broadway and saw *The Great White*

Way which I had heard so much about. I was up all night running the streets with Horace; it was my first time seeing New York City at night. The lights were breathtaking, everything seemed to be illuminated. The next day, Horace took me to Coney Island and to the movie houses. I saw all types of movies; I had never been in such large theatres. He took me to Botanical Gardens in Brooklyn which reminded me of some of the gardens in Florida. Horace took me on trips using the subway and he taught me how to buy and use tokens. I fell in love with New York City; the sights, sounds, people, and the skyscrapers. I had never seen so many people or buildings in my life!

Horace left me with his Aunt Mae when he had to return to the base. While he was away, I got directions on how to get to 42nd street in Manhattan. When I got there, I was content just following the crowds. I didn't know where they were going, everybody was rushing to get to their destinations and I rushed right along side of them. This left me confused because crowds would separate as everyone went their own way. I wondered around and found Fifth Avenue along with Park and Madison avenues. I had heard about those avenues before.

Riding the subway was something I learned by doing repeatedly. At first, I thought that one token meant that you could ride, get off, go outside, come back in and ride some more without using another token. When I was ready to return to Brooklyn, I went back into the train station but I was unsure as to how I was going to get back in since I used my token. I went under the turnstile and it was then that someone told me I had to buy a new token every time I entered the subway. Horace had taught me about tokens but some things weren't clear and I never thought to ask. I found the train that I needed and returned to Brooklyn.

Horace returned from the base that weekend. This was to be the last weekend before I entered the convent. We had a good time hanging out on the New York City streets. The next day Horace and I left his Aunt's house to go to the convent. We got there and I rang the bell. It seemed like it took forever for someone to come to the door but finally a nun, clad in black, stood in the entrance of the door smiling and bidding us to enter. She took Horace and me down to a small parlor and left us. The floor had a beautiful shiny wood finish that you could see your own face. The room had simple furniture, a few chairs and a table along with a picture of Jesus on the wall. There was a beautiful flower arrangement on the table and the walls were covered in wallpaper with a floral pattern. It was a peaceful room; I looked out the window to see a park across the street which I later found out to be Mount Morris Park. I was talking to Horace about the beauty of the room when a Sister came in.

"Hello," she said welcoming us, "Are you two hungry?"

"Yes" we responded in unison.

The Sister escorted us down a long hall leading to an adjacent building. We were seated in a large parlor where we waited to eat. When the Sister came back, she took us to a dining room where we sat waiting patiently with napkins in our laps. We were served salad, baked chicken with mixed vegetables, dinner rolls, milk, and Jell-o for dessert. When we finished Horace noticed that it was time for him to leave. He anticipated a long ride back to the base and wanted to get there before nightfall. I told him that I wanted him to stay longer. He explained that it was impossible to stay any longer. He also told me that if this was the last time seeing me, he had enjoyed the time that we spent together. He told me that he would always remember me and that he wanted me to always remember him as well.

"Will you come and get me if I don't like this place?" I said.

"Of course I will Delois" he replied.

He felt confident that I would like it at the convent; the nuns seemed to be so nice. He gave me his number and said to call him if anything went wrong.

A nun came into the parlor and discussed my getting a bath and rest because I needed to prepare for the next day. I asked the nun if I could walk Horace to the door and she said yes. Horace and I went downstairs to the front door where we hugged and said farewell. I asked him to pray for me and to write to me. That moment was very perplexing because part of me wanted to leave the convent and look for an apartment in New York City. Reality had finally set in. I had been introduced to the convent, met some of the nuns and now I was unsure about my decision. Horace reassured me about my decision. He told me that I was doing the right thing and that there was nothing to be anxious about, and with that, Horace was gone.

I went back upstairs and the sister was there waiting and smiling. She introduced me to some of the girls that were my age in that particular building. When I saw so many others like me I was relieved. Overcome with happiness now knowing that other girls my age were at the convent, I asked the girls if all of them were entering the convent like me. They said that they weren't, they were apart of a special boarding school which was housed in the same building as the nuns' dormitory. I have to say I was a little disappointed but, I felt proud that I awed all of the girls by my entering the convent at their age.

That night I stayed in the home for the girls. We talked and watched television and played games. The girls talked to me about the nuns; they said that they liked them. Some of the girls had been sent to the school by the courts for constant truancy at school. Some were orphans and others were working girls. It was very interesting being there with girls from various backgrounds sharing life experiences. I shared a room with the girls so, later on when it was time to go to bed, (the nuns made sure that we went to bed on time) we talked long into the night. We finally drifted off to sleep in the wee hours. The next morning, I awoke to find everyone up and getting ready for school or work. We had breakfast together; cereal, fruit, eggs, bacon, toast, tea and coffee. I got ready and waited.

A nun came to get me and told me we were going to the Novitiate house—a convent house on Staten Island. We prepared to enter a green station wagon for our trip. It was then that I realized all of the nuns, except myself, Sister Ursula, and Mother Eugenia, were black with high yellow complexions. We left from 124th street in what I later was told was "Harlem," and headed for Penn Station to pick up my trunk. As we pulled off from in front of the building I looked at the structure; red brick, grayish green steps, and a dark green door. The car weaved in and out of traffic as we drove to the train station. Mother Eugenia had my baggage claim check and presented it to the clerk. I remember how kindly and cordially everyone treated the nuns as we got my luggage and left Penn Station.

Chapter Eight: Early Days at the Convent

While we were headed to Staten Island I recall Mother Eugenia pointing out the streets, important places, and buildings. I listened to her talk about certain areas of Manhattan. At first I didn't know the difference between New York City and the borough of Manhattan I thought it was its own separate city. The station wagon was driven onto the Staten Island ferry. When we went over the narrow bridge to get on and off the ferry, the sisters made the sign of the cross and observing them, I did the same thing. The sisters said silent prayers while we were headed to Staten Island. It was a long journey to the convent. During the last mile to my destiny, I was in reflection of my past experiences.

We left the waterfront area and began to go through neighborhoods around curved and hilly roads; one was a rather large section of the trip. Mother Eugenia busied herself with her prayers and some of the other nuns followed suit. The next part of the trip went over a lonely road on which we were the only car. The nuns told me that it was called Hylan Boulevard. There was nothing but wood and trees on both sides of the road, it was early fall and the scenery was beautiful. The air was scented with apples from the nearby trees and there was not a single person to be seen. I then started thinking how isolated the convent must be. It seemed like we rode for hours on this particular road.

We turned onto another road which carried us even further into the woods. We made many turns and went deeper into the woods when at last I saw a large white house. There were beautiful flowers and gardens around the house; the lawn stretched up a hill where a statue of a crucifix and the stations of prayer were represented by an outdoor sculpture. There were many other cars belonging to other people who were inside the building, perhaps waiting for us. There was a huge fence around the Novitiate house. At the front of the house was a lake and, in the back of the house, the Stations of the Cross led to the highway. As we road towards the house, the driver of the station wagon blew the horn. From the building came many nuns to greet us.

"Praise be to Jesus and Mother Mary" said the nuns to each other and the car we traveled in.

"Now and forever, Sister" replied Mother Eugenia. They all came up to the car we were in and proceeded to help us, carrying the various packages from the car.

Sister Ursula and Mother Eugenia were very happy to see them. Mother Eugenia had an olive complexion; she could pass for someone from the Mediterranean. She was a little on the old side, heavy-set, wore glasses, and spoke with a slow and drowsy cadence. But, when she laughed it was always hearty. What distinguished her was the beauty of her smile and her calm, slow manner. Sister Ursula was also on the old side and heavy-set. She was olive skinned as well, and her most distinguishing characteristic was that she muffled her words when she spoke. Sister Ursula simply could not speak well. She talked pretty fast to begin with and since she was an old sister, she was out of breath quickly. But she was vivacious and worked hard. Both Sister Ursula and Mother Eugenia had ridden with me in the station wagon and Sister Ursula wished me well because she was about to leave us and proceed across the road to the camp. Mother Eugenia and I went into the Novitiate house through the back door and went up the back stair case to the main floor.

At the top of the stairs, there were two halls leading in opposite directions. The left hall led to the kitchen and the dining room. The right hall led to the various parlors, the chapel and cloister, and the hall to the front door. Opposite the front door was the chapel and both the front door and the chapel opened into the vestibule. Inside the chapel door was the cloister. I noticed that one inside the cloister the sisters changed their voices they spoke very softly. I told the sister who was with me that I wished to be taken to my room. She whispered back that I was being taken to my cell. "My cell...What do you mean my *cell*?!" I exclaimed.

It was later explained to me that a cell was a room. I was escorted to my cell by a young nun. She was the novice mistress which meant she was a little older than the nuns who had come out of the house to greet Mother Eugenia and me when we arrived. We went further to the back and the sister instructed me to change clothes. She helped me to get into the nun clothes I had brought along, she wasn't aware that I had practiced getting into the clothes so, it was rather easy for me to get dressed. I discovered that I also had to change from the briefs that I was wearing into the long Johns which the nuns wear. The Sister made sure that I had completely taken off all the old clothes and that the only clothes that I wore were the new articles that were part of the nun's outfit. As final touches were put on, the nun helped me adjust my hair for the head piece I was to wear. Then she placed the veil on my head. The final touch was the stiff white collar she placed around my neck and the stiff white cardboard cuffs that went around my wrists.

With all that done, the nun told me to go with her. I went with her to another room where she and I found two other girls who were becoming nuns at the same time as I was. This sister was dressing them as well. One girl named Rita was from the Virgin Islands. She had a high yellow complexion. The other future nun was Sherry and she was from Philadelphia. She too was very light skinned. I still hadn't seen any dark-skinned blacks there. Everyone was high yellow and as we went into the convent, I began to wonder what kind of convent I was in. It was altogether impossible to say how "black" these Sisters and girls were simply by looking at them.

None of them had black characteristics; noses or lips. Absent from my analysis of their racial compositions was the texture of hair since the nun's habit completely covered the hair. We never saw more than each others faces because our bodies were always completely covered

I thought I had been sent to a racially mixed convent, but I wasn't sure. Later, we all went into a large room and it was confirmed that I was the darkest one there, truly a fly in buttermilk. There were no close seconds, thirds or fourths. Everyone in that room had skin so light; some could even pass for white women. Without being able to see anything other than a face, I couldn't say that it was a black convent like I had been led to believe. For a while I thought that my papers got mixed up and I had been sent to the wrong convent. I thought that eventually someone would discover the error, find me missing from their enrollees and come to get me. Perhaps if I was able to see some kinky hair I would have accepted the fact that I was sent to a black convent sooner.

I finally settled the matter in my mind; I concluded that it was a black convent, as I had hoped, by listening to the others speak. Rita spoke with a strange accent. She spoke like a person we called

"Geechee." In Florida, we had the Geechees from the Bahamas so I instantly recognized the style of Rita's speech. Sherry from Philadelphia spoke very "proper," not at all like the others. I noticed that the nuns in the convent spoke differently from me; they all spoke like the northerners they were. All the Neophytes and the Sisters of the convent were seated in the large room waiting for the sister to come and get us. While we waited, we conversed among each other. Sister Veronica, the Novice Mistress finally arrived and took us back to the chapel. At the chapel, we were able to spend time with any relatives that brought us to the convent, as was the case with Rita and Sherry. Sherry's entire family had driven her there that morning; they were waiting in the parlor. Sherry's parents were both high yellow. Rita's aunt turned out to be white and she was also waiting in the chapel. I later found out that Rita was of mixed parentage; black father and a white mother. Her father had a high yellow complexion as well.

Me? Well, I had no one waiting in the chapel. I busied myself by going to the front of the convent and looking around at the front lawn and the beach. All of a sudden, a bell rang. One of the nuns with the white veil, a Novice, was clanging away. She came to the door and beckoned me to come inside. I went inside the convent and the Sister indicated for me to go right into the chapel. She placed the three of us exactly where she wanted us to be. I was placed near the front; Sherry was placed right next to me. Rita was placed behind me and another nun was placed next to Rita. There were two of us in a pew and two on a bench on both sides of the aisle. Then, the Novice gave us our prayer books to be placed in our pews. When that was done we all knew our permanent places in the chapel.

The Sisters started praying. They were praying the afternoon prayers. She rang the second bell and everybody began. They started praying very fast. All I could do was listen to them. After they said the Mattars and Lords prayers, they cited the rosary. The newcomers knew the rosary so it was here we chimed in. Of course the newcomers did not know the routine; we had to look at the experienced nuns in order to know when to stand and when to kneel. It was intriguing; the kneeling and the standing, changing sides and chanting, but it was still awkward for us newcomers. The Novice Mistress came for us. She showed us how to leave the chapel; there was a certain way it was done, making the sign of the cross and leaving. In the later months we all leaned how to do those things. When we left, Rita and Sherry's relatives were still there waiting in the chapel. I was left alone again and decided to wander around the building for the time being.

At 6:00 P.M. it was time for the relatives to leave. While they were all saying their goodbyes, I went back into the cloister and took a seat. There were novice nuns in the room who began to talk to me. They welcomed me, saying they were happy to have me. We had a short conversation while I waited Rita and Sherry. I heard them clopping down the hall in their nun shoes and I was happy to hear that sound. I felt comfortable with Rita and Sherry who were as I was—unlearned about so many aspects of life.

When they came into the room, we greeted each other and it was then that we were labeled a band. Of our new band of three, Rita was the oldest, Sherry was the second oldest, and I was the youngest at 16 years old. While my band and I were talking together a big bell was sounded, it was very loud. A nun came into the vestibule ringing the bell. She would clang, the bell on one side of the hallway, and clang, clang, clang the bell on the other side of the hallway. The Sisters who were in the room told us that the ringing of the bell was the call of God, it was the sound of God calling us to prayer. "What is this? Praying again?" I thought to myself. "They pray *all* the time."

All of the nuns left the room and we went up the dark hall that led into the vestibule where the chapel was. We did not go into the chapel immediately. They lined us up outside the door. We got on our knees. I was keeping an eye on the experienced nuns to see what they were doing. Then another high yellow Sister who looked white said, "In the name of the Father, the Son, and the Holy Spirit." They started what they called the Angela. The nun who was speaking said some more words and the other sisters answered her. I thought the other bells were loud but suddenly, I was shaken by a bell which seemed to vibrate everything in the building. The sound came from somewhere in the ceiling.

"CLUNG...CLUNG...CLUNG..." the bell sounded. "What is going on?" I said to myself. It was as if a fire alarm had gone off because the only time I remembered hearing a bell that loud, was when a building was engulfed in flames. The nun creating the sound was pulling a big, heavy rope that led to the attic. I turned every which way to see what was happening. I thought the whole surrounding area was going to run into the convent. You could hear the echo inside and outside the building; the nun was putting all her weight on the rope. The nuns started saying a prayer and I started mumbling something I thought sounded like what they were saying. They said the prayer three times and when the prayers finished the bell still sounded. I was dying to see where the bell was or how far up in the attic it was located. When that bell ringing was over, a sister started ringing another bell, a hand bell located by the chapel. The sounds of the bells resounded in my ears. My band did not know what was happening or what was about to happen so we stood there staring at each other in confusion.

The Sister Novice has us wait when a processional started. Mother Eugenia was first, then the older nuns and Sister Veronica. The Sister who did the cooking, Sister Anthony-Marie was next. If there were any visiting Sister in the convent, they went in afterwards. Sister Ursula had gone across the street, so she was not there. There were other Sisters who went in next that I had not seen before. They went in; the novice Sisters held us newcomers until the end. I was the last one in the line. I was not sure how they decided on the order of our band, but I figured it had to do with the age since I was the youngest one.

We all marched down a hallway into a room which looked like a dining room. In the room there were long tables on both sides of the room. There was also a table in the center of the room. At the center table sat the Novice Sister, the sister in charge of the convent, Mother Eugenia and another senior Sister. The guest sisters sat on the side. All the novices sat at the side tables and we were able to see all the young sisters sitting across from each other. Altogether, there were about twelve Sisters assembled. Before we could eat, we stood facing the crucifix and said, "In the name of the Father, the Son, and the Holy Spirit." We made the sign of the cross and Mother Eugenia led us in the blessing of the food. I noticed that the novices waited until the senior nuns sat down. When that was done, they signaled for the rest of us to sit. One of the novices sat down and began to read. All of a sudden someone said, "Dominus Nobiscus." The whole room shouted, "Deo Gracius, Mother" meaning "thanks be to God."

This was to be a celebration, so there was no reading that night. The younger Sisters were lifting the food that was to be served at the head table. The head table was served by the junior Sisters and the younger Sisters. At the table of the younger Sisters, the food was simply passed around. This was my first meal with the nuns. I was busy watching how they were going to eat. The senior nuns placed their napkins on their laps. The meal consisted of roast beef, potatoes, string beans; pie and cake were for dessert. Salad, fruit, milk, and water were on the table along with the bread and butter. It was all very tasty.

After eating everyone was eager to hear what Mother Eugenia had to say. When she spoke it was soft and low. Mother Eugenia told us stories from her experiences and news from the city. She had visited the uptown neighborhoods and was reporting everything back to us. At that time, I did not know that the place where I had been picked up from was Harlem. I learned more about the community as I continued living there. Those at the dinner wanted to hear from Mother Eugenia about the Sisters in the Harlem convent. They wanted to know how they were doing, what activities they were involved in, and about the missions of the order; would there be any more nurses or teachers? Mother Eugenia informed us of what was happening on the social level of the order.

When everyone had finished eating, we collected the dishes where we were given aprons and shown what to do. We worked as a team to wash the dishes. This task was not done by the senior Sisters, the young novices and postulates performed this chore. When we finished the cleaning of the dishes, a small bell sounded. "Ting, Ting…" the Sister who was instructing us in our kitchen duties told us that the bell was a signal to go. We folded our aprons quickly and left the room. We were instructed to return to the table where we had dined. We entered the room to find all the sisters turned toward the crucifix.

"In the name of the Father and the Son, and Holy Spirit, we give thanks for the meal we have just received"

"Ooh…*another prayer*" I said to myself.

The group of us moved from the room still reciting the prayer and headed towards the chapel. We prayed down the hall and into the chapel. When we entered the chapel, I saw that we extended our arms to pray this time. There was more recitation and prayers. Then there were more prayers while our arms were still extended. The prayer was repeated for a period of time while we knelt at our places in the pews. We made the sign of the cross and bowed our heads.

We stoop up, made the sign of the cross again and marched out of the chapel in formation. I just experienced a little of the total regimen in a nun's life.

We left the chapel and headed for the community room where we all sat down. A sister stood in front of us and informed us that we were getting ready to see a special play. The special play was to welcome me, Rita, and Sherry. At once, people got busy rearranging the room. We all waited around for Mother Eugenia to enter the room with the Novice Mistress, and the visiting nuns. At that time I did not know how important to the nuns Mother Eugenia was in convent life. She was in charge of most things in the convent and everyone loved her. She was simple and very quiet in her manner. I often wondered why some of us were Sisters and others were Mothers when it occurred to me that the titles had to do with the description of duties in the convent.

At last the preparations for the play were completed. A sister stood in front of us and began to speak.

"We welcome Sister Rita, Sister Sherry, and Sister Dee-Lois," mispronouncing my name like so many others. *They don't even know my name*...I thought to myself. She proceeded to welcome Mother

113

Eugenia, Mother Dorothy, and Sister Veronica, and everyone else there. "Now we shall give our play to you," she continued.

While they performed their skit, my mind wandered back to Fort Lauderdale. I wondered what they were doing and what was happening. How was my town? How were the kids at school? Most importantly, how were my Daddy, my sisters, and Mu'Dear? While they were skipping across the stage I had no idea what they were doing—something about a saint. It was boring to me whatever it was. The idea of a saint was new to me and I must say, I didn't see the relevance to the arrival of the new Sisters in the convent. My knowledge of what they were referring to was limited it was like a new language to me.

I was still day dreaming when I was awakened by the applause for the players. I jolted upright and clapped like I was on the case. When the play was over, the sister announced that she would like Sister Rita to get up and do something for the audience. So Sister Rita, who grinned the whole time she was performing, got up and recited a short Catholic poem. She had a silly grin, she was nervous and even turned a little red; I could tell she was scared. We all clapped for her. Then it was time for Sister Sherry to perform. She

114

was nervous too. She said with a nervous laugh that she didn't know what to do but she would try something. It was another Catholic poem; light and modest. When Sherry finished Sister Elaine said "And last but not least, we are happy to have Sister Dee-Lois share her talents with us." I said that I also did not know what to do but I would attempt to sing the Lord's Prayer. So, I folded my hands in front of me and stood with perfect posture. I noticed the piano, but I didn't ask if any one would play, I sang A-capella. In my best operatic voice, I sang the Lord's Prayer. I knew I had a lovely contralto voice and when I finished singing they all clapped. My song ended the program.

The bell sounded for us to return to prayer again. During that prayer time, there was silent time which was used for meditation. The chapel was very quiet. The bell rang and Mother Eugenia said a few words. The chapel became very quiet for about a half-hour. After that it was time to chant the night prayer and close to 9:00 p.m. another bell rang. The 9:00p.m. bell signaled silence which would last until the next day. The lighting in the hallway was very dim now. The older Sisters guided us to our cells and when I entered it for the second time since I got there I looked around a bit. It had one window, a single bed which was dark brass and one dark brown nightstand. On the nightstand was a basin for water, a small picture of the Savior and a statue. There was a crucifix on the wall; there weren't any mirrors in the room. At the foot of the bed, there was a dark brown metal closet for clothing. Next to the wall was a shelf for folded garments and other personal belongings.

There was one brown chair next to the door. Next to the nightstand was where we were to place our Bibles, the Missal which is a prayer book similar to the Bible, rosaries, and crown; the seven joys of our Lady, the Blessed Virgin Mary, mother of Jesus. Instead of saying our rosaries we had to say the Francisca Crown; the seven joys of our Lady. On the nightstand was a simple desk light, and on the bed was a simple bed spread.

That was my room. There were simple white curtains at the windows—everything was simple! While in my room I looked around it trying to make an adjustment. It was difficult for me to start undressing in this new room and new place. The austerity of the room made me shiver a little. The room had all the features of my not belonging there. It was bare, this was not my room. Companionship was missing. This was more austere than the

Harlem convent where I spent the first night. I imagined that across the hall from me was the same type of room. I heard the doors close up and down the hall. The nuns were entering a oneness with themselves. In that room I felt neither the beauty, nor the presence of God. In that room, God seemed cold, strange, and distant. The room did not inspire my feelings for a warm, compassionate God. Besides that, I was alone.

While I was coping with my emotions, there came a tap on the door, a soft sound. The door knob turned while I sat there on my bed with all my clothes on.

"Praise be to Jesus and Mother Mary," said Sister Veronica smiling beautifully upon entering my room. Sister Veronica had brought warmth and I smiled back. My smile told her that I did not know how to respond.

"What shall I do now?" I asked.

She said that it was time for bed. She sprinkled water on my bed and some on me. The water was ice cold and yelped. She shushed me and reminded me that it was silent time, "grand silence time," she whispered.

"Why did you sprinkle that cold water on me?" I asked.

"It's holy water," she responded continuing to sprinkle water on everything in the room, including the walls and the floor.

Sister Veronica smiled when she finished and left the room.

After she had closed my door, I could hear the swish of her habit and the shaking of her beads. She left me with a great feeling of warmth—the first I had experienced in the convent. Now, the sound of her footsteps faded down the hall as she made her rounds with the holy water. The sound of her footsteps and beads became louder as she proceeded back toward my cell. I was thirsty and I wanted to know where I could get the water for my basin. She informed me that it was also time for me to draw the water from the bathroom and instructed me where to go.

I moved into the hall and observed the other Sisters who had already changed into their gowns and bathrobes. I had put on the gown, but had forgotten to put on the robe. The Novice Sister observed me and told me to return to my cell for my robe. I remembered that the other Sisters had also put on their night veils. Everything was white; the gown, the robe, and the veil. I did not have anything for my head except for a red handkerchief which had belonged to my mother. I put the handkerchief on my head, picked up my pail, and proceeded to walk to the bathroom.

In the bathroom I observed many showers and many basins. I asked a Sister there if I should shower and she said, "No, fill your pail and return to your cell." I was also told that in the morning I would have to use the water for washing up. This all seemed very confusing. I saw some other sisters so I waved and they waved back. This part of our routine seemed a little friendlier but I still had to look forward to sleeping in the barren cell alone. As I approached my cell, a bell rang. A sister nearby informed me that the bell signaled it was time to turn off the lights. When I turned off my light, it was pitch blackness. I decided I did not want to fall asleep in pitch darkness so I parted the curtains, raised the window shade all the way up and cracked the door so I could get some of the dim light coming from the hall. This was the first time I had been isolated in this way from people. I was isolated from sounds coming from within and without the house. This seemed like an icy existence. Why couldn't the room have the scents of sweet smells like flowers, or perfumes? "Then again," I thought, "the room *is* called a cell…"

There was no dainty lamp, no ruffled dressing table, just metal, plaster and tiles resembling asphalt on the floor. When I think of God I think of goodness, beauty, warmth, loving, and kindness. All these attributes of God were missing from this room. This was a room in which I would worship God and spend the rest of my life, in this naked cell. I laid myself on the bed and began to cry. I asked God to protect me; I asked him to protect me from the feelings of loneliness, and to protect my family from all harm, danger, and evil. For some reason I was unable to understand I was afraid to kneel on the floor. I knelt on my bed facing away from the big metal closet which looked frightening in the dark. I covered my head with the blanket and in this position, I prayed. I thought that the Sisters were in some way strange, and I did not know what to expect. For some reason at this time, I did not see the nuns as good people.

I remembered from reading religious books how the young were often sacrificed. It occurred to me that I was going to be the one sacrificed because I was always put at the end of the line every time we did anything or made processionals. I thought of how Abraham was about to sacrifice his son. I thought to myself that maybe this was the way you were treated before you were sacrificed. I thought that they would want to burn me at the stake, or do something harmful. I prayed to God that I would not be the first one to be sacrificed. I said to God that I loved him and wanted to sacrifice my life for him, but please, don't let the sacrifice be painful. I told God that I didn't want to be like Sister Laura back in Fort Lauderdale, I didn't want to be a nun anymore I just wanted to go home. If he would let me go home I would be good. He would not have to worry about my doing anything wrong if I could go home. I would live as a good Christian. I prayed to leave the convent; between tears and prayers, the thoughts of sixteen year old mind lulled me to sleep.

I was awakened by a bell. The bell was loud and I jumped up startled. I looked out the window, it was still dark outside.

Why are we ringing bells in the middle of the night? What's it for anyway? I thought to myself.

"Benictus de Mino!" The loud call resounded up and down the hallway which translated "Thanks be to God!" in English.

"Deo Gracius" was the response, the same call and response I heard at dinner, I now heard from every nun in their cell. Then I heard Sisters hitting the floor, something I had not heard before. There was a tap on the door, a senior Sister who wanted to be sure I was up and okay. She told me to dress quickly and that she would return.

When I was ready to brush my teeth, I was told to use the water in my basin. I used a cup that was on the nightstand to rinse my mouth out after brushing my teeth. I remembered the cold holy water that the nun had thrown on me the night before as I washed up in the cold water from the pail. I had never washed with cold water before and my first morning in the convent left me thinking that it was the worst experience I had ever had. I began to believe that the convent was full of mean women. I asked one of the nuns if I could have warm water and she refused. There were no explanations about these practices; they simply wanted us to follow them. Blind obedience is what they wanted. I had never been one to follow orders blindly but I did what I was told. This was a new challenge for me; I couldn't ask questions and everything was communicated in hushed tones or complete silence.

Every time I asked something no one replied. They indicated that everything had to be done quickly. The nun returned and told me to quickly remove the sheets and blanket from my bed and to fold them and place them on my chair. It was as if a fire was moving through the building. The nun then commanded me to turn up the mattress. The mattress was difficult to move. It was heavy and I had never done a lot of heavy lifting. Waking up before daylight and turning up mattress was not apart of my daily routine, I mean, did they really expect me to do all of this after I just washed up in ice cold water? Nonetheless, I did what I was told. The nun then instructed me to raise the window as high as I could and I did so. The cold dew and frigid air came rushing at me full force. What was with these nuns and their affinity for the cold?

I didn't know what time it was. It seemed like I had just fallen asleep when the bell rang waking me up. Another bell rang.

"Leave your cell and go to the chapel quickly, quickly!" The nun commanded.

"Alright, alright," I responded wearily.

I rushed out of my cell still trying to put my veil in place. I forgot my cuffs and had to run back to my cell. I ran down the hallway making quite a bit of noise with my clunky, old fashioned, senior-citizen shoes. I rushed down to the chapel, made the sign of the cross and heard another bell ring.

CLANG…CLANG…CLANG…CLANG… the bell resounded.

"In the name of the Father, the Son, and the Holy Spirit," I heard Mother Dorothy say from the back of the chapel.

We were responsible for being there on time and if we were really late arriving we were punished.

I tried to follow the prayers. I noticed the stained glass windows for the first time since I had arrived yesterday. I took a closer look at the chapel and I saw the candles; the only source of light. It was still dark outside. *Why are they doing this to us?* I thought to myself. As we continued our prayers, "Glory be to God; the Father, the Son, and the Holy Spirit."

"As it was in the beginning, is now and ever shall be…world without end, Amen" I said as my head was bowed.
The chanting of the other prayers began. There was a leader on one side of the aisle and the chorus that responded on the other side. The role of leader went back and forth between aisles and the chanting went was nonstop. I thought the Sisters would never end their chanting. It seemed as if all they wanted to do was pray, pray, and pray some more.

"I love God but do we have to pray this much?" I asked myself. At this point I realized how little I knew about the nunnery.

"God, I vowed to love you and to serve you but I didn't know that this is what life would be like here. I love you very much God, please show me the way."

My prayer was not the prayer which the nuns were reciting. They prayed in Latin and I only was able to understand a few words.

As the sister continued to pray, an elderly priest came in. He could barely make it down the aisle. I could not believe that he was so old he could barely move. The elderly priest looked strange. He was white; hunched over, and had snow white hair. He walked painstakingly slow to the altar. He had to turn his whole body when he made gestures; he had very limited mobility of his neck and arms. The priest was nearly deaf and spoke very loudly. He did not sound like he was from the north or the south and his accent was strange. I later found out that he was a foreigner from Europe, Lithuania I believe I heard someone say. His name was strange as well, Father Gerafa. The Sister who lit the candles understood him. She worked with the sacraments in the sanctuary. She was the one who laid out the priest's vestment. She helped him dress and I must admit I was a little bit afraid of him.

At this time, the Sisters began to take out their Hymn books and Sister Veronica began playing the organ. I was very sleepy at this point, and I didn't know whether to fall asleep or stay awake. We were all on our knees and I decided to try and sleep but the organ kept me awake. The bell rang again. This was to announce mass but to whom? We were already assembled, why did they ring the bell again? I guess they just liked ringing them. It was time to start Mass. The priest began it but it took him a long time to kneel and make the sign of the cross. I thought the poor man would kneel and would not be able to get up again. But he did don't ask me how! He continued Mass and I thought that he would die before he was able to finish. It occurred to me later that he would not die during Mass so I decided to pay attention to what he was saying. I forgot about the priest being old and possibly witnessing his death on the altar due to complications with his age. We started singing; I knew I had a lovely voice and I concentrated on the singing trying my best to forget how sleepy I was.

Chapter Nine: The Nun In Training

Father Gerafa very slowly turned after he finished mass and the bell was rung signaling the last supper; the breaking of the bread and drinking of the wine. At that point I became nostalgic for my church in Fort Lauderdale and felt close to the sanctuary of the convent. I began to see that the same Jesus that I had served in Fort Lauderdale at the Annunciation Church was the same Jesus I would serve in the convent. At that point I became very happy. I was able to bridge the distance between the two experiences. With that revelation, Jesus became my true friend. A comforter to me, he became a very close friend; I talked with him all the time. I walked with him also. I began to unfold a certain type of happiness in the convent. Not looking so much at the coldness of the place or what the sisters said or did not say, I began to appreciate a little of the convent life because now, I was in communication with the Jesus I knew.

After receiving Holy Communion, I promised Jesus that if he would be my friend, I would love him forever. I remembered that when the priest placed the body of Christ on my tongue, he was trembling. I thought that Christ would never ever tremble. I enraptured myself at that moment in the body of Christ. From that moment on, I carried Christ within me; my heart, my daily activities, and in my life. As I carried Christ with me, my life in the convent began to change. I no longer relied on what the sisters were doing or not doing, or what they said or did not say. I knew now why I was there and that I had come of my own free-will. It had nothing to do with the sisters or the building called the convent. They were there I am sure, for the same reason I was there. We were different women who had the love of Jesus in common. With that awareness, I began to understand what was happening in my life. As we moved through the chapel, I had a new spirit within me. An inner strength, and an inner belonging with the environment; it enveloped me.

Blessing our food and spiritual reading became a daily routine. In the refectory, our dining room, we all faced the crucifix to pray. We ate in complete silence. I was now prepared for a life of quietude with God. Hearing the scriptures and beginning my studies of the word, added to my comfort. Everyday we studied the way to be a good Christian; the way to become the bride of Christ. One must learn the ways of oneself; all postulants had to know themselves and learn the ways of Christ in order to be Christ' bride. Everyday we began to learn our basic prayers. We began to learn what sacrifice truly meant—why did we get up so early? Why did we wash in cold water? Why did we have silence? It was all in order to spend time with Christ, to learn more about the bridegroom to be. All the things we did were beginning to have meaning. We studied to learn more about the bridegroom and we also learned what we needed to get rid of in order to welcome the bridegroom.

I came to know the schedule: arise at 5:20 a.m. then, Angela would ring at 6:00 a.m. for us to assemble in the chapel. We then went into Morning Prayer. After Morning Prayer, we went into meditation. Meditation time is when you are one with God. You kneel or sit in silence. You must take one basic thought. At first it was very difficult for me to discipline myself to concentrate. But given time, I mastered the skills of meditation and prayer.

Meditation became something very close to me. I began to yearn for meditation time, the time when I was one with God. I began to yearn for the periods of silence in my life. There was a time to talk and a time to be still. There was a time to plant and a time to pluck. When I began to see that there was a time and a season for all things, I began to put my religious life in a time and season frame of reference. I began to use part of the scriptures as my way of life and as a way of looking at my religious life. There was a time to pray, a time for meditation, a time for recreation, a time for work and a time for rest during the day. An average nun's day was like that. There was a set time for everything. My life was divided and parts were set aside for all the various tasks she had to be part of. I remember there was even a time for singing.

Whatever we did we strived for the "perfect" day; every minute of everyday, we tried to be perfect. So whatever we did, whether it was cleaning the bathroom or preparing the meal, oiling down the Oakwood banister or cleaning the stained glass in the chapel, scrubbed the floor on hands and knees or buffed them to make them shine, we gave our hearts and souls to excellence in service.

Every task was done for the honor and glory of God. What we were taught to do was to give our best to God; perfection became a way of life for me. Each day I vowed to give God my best. When the bell rang it was the will of God, it was God calling me. So, at the sound of the bell, we dropped everything and answered the bell as it was God calling us to join whatever activity was taking place at that time. Even recreation time was performed for the Love of God, whether it was going out to play volleyball, or basketball, or going for a long walk in the park or on the beach.

We were taught that God is the priority in life and that we should rid ourselves of anything which was not of God. We were taught about our character. I will always remember when Sister Veronica described my character as sociable, and determined to have things my way. Sister Veronica felt that I had the makings of a great person; a great person to a nun is a saint. She said I had the same personality that could also make me a great sinner. I could go from one extreme to the other; a choice everyone makes in life. Sister Veronica also said I had a will of my own. She saw that my will needed to be broken and molded in order for me to serve God. She constantly told me the things that I needed to get rid of.

"You should not be stubborn," she would say. "When told to do something, don't ask why you have to do it, just do it." "You must do the will of God without questioning the will of God." That was how I would build saintliness and be the perfect person.

Sister Veronica told me about my issues with pride. She said I wanted to lead everyone else. I was told to curb those characteristics. I had to learn to follow. She said that I was quite argumentative and I told her, "You do not know me so how can you possibly say all those things about me?" She said it was her duty and responsibility to mold me and train a postulant; to make me into a bride of Christ. It was her duty to tell me my strengths and weaknesses. I then explained to her that what she saw as my weaknesses I saw as my strengths. Those characteristics were what made me love God. Those characteristics were what brought me to the convent. How could she tell me to get rid of them?

"No," said Sister Veronica, "I am not trying to get you to rid yourself of those characteristics, I am simply telling you to take the perfect parts of yourself, and that positive energy within you that can be cultivated."

"This is all very confusing" I said.

"You should try to be more humble," she told me.

"I will try to be more humble," I replied.

I found myself trying to be something I was not. I was not docile; I could not walk around whispering when I wanted to speak in my normal voice. I could not pretend to be modest when I was really friendly and outgoing; when I knew I could do things well why did I have to appear to be otherwise? The things that I needed to improve upon, I would; I knew that I was not God. As I left Sister Veronica, I remember taking what she had to say very, very seriously.

Chapter Ten: Convent Blues

I remember Sister Veronica reading to us one morning; she reported that God liked simplicity and humility. That morning I took this as my meditation. I asked God to teach me humility—show me humility. I prayed and meditated for weeks on just humility alone, asking God to help me become humble and not to be a proud individual.

Sister Veronica continued, "Hell was created by the pride of angels—Satan." I thought it was a very awful thing to say. Why would I want to be proud and be like Satan? I left the warmth of family, friends, and neighbors just to be told that because of my pride I could end up like Satan! That's all I needed to hear, I was more confused than ever. If I had given up so much for God including my virginity just to end up like Satan, something was definitely wrong. Did I want to be the bride of Christ or Satan? Was Sister Veronica telling the truth? Was this the place I belonged?

As I remember, after meditation I went into the community room where we were allowed to talk. We were not permitted to speak in most of the other places of the building.

"Sister I have a problem that I must work on based on what Sister Veronica said," quickly starting the conversation.

"What? What is the problem?" The Sister replied.

"Wait, wait first give me a sheet of paper," I then asked her to turn around. On the sheet of paper I wrote "humility." I then took the paper with the word on it, placed it on the floor and stood on it.

"What, what is it?" She asked turning around.

"I must learn," I stepped off of the piece of paper revealing the word, she laughed.

"You can never learn the meaning of humility by standing on the word," she said.

"I must practice humility by standing on the word itself" I explained. "I must ask God to make me humble from the feet up."

"No, no, no! She doesn't mean it *that* way she means that you must work on your attitudes and how to treat others. It's the way you treat others, how you behave, and what you do. You must ask God to let him be first. You must practice humility in your own simple way."

I was very glad that she gave me humility from another point of view. It was a life-time job as this nun saw it. Humility is something that you practice. Humility means that you hold God above everyone else. She began to explain to me what humility meant as a virtue, and I began to read more. The convent had many, many books in its library. I asked the Sister to help me pick out books containing humility and similar virtues which Christ would want in his bride. Through that, I got a better understanding.

One day in the library, the Sister pointed out a saint; Saint Tereasa of Avala. She handed me the book and said, "Read this." I found in reading it that Saint Tereasa of Avala was somewhat like me. She was sociable, a good leader, and liked traveling. She liked being involved in things and even told God off! She talked to God like he was her true friend and she helped people.

She became my model saint, Saint Tereasa, the go-getter. She reminded me of women of the south. She reminded me of my own great-aunt; outgoing and ambitious. Saint Tereasa had a profession and was in control of her life. Yes, I wanted to be Tereasa of Avala, fighting the war of Christ and becoming Joan of Arc. I aspired to be like the strong-willed women I read about, a woman who would fight and hold up the banner of God. Women like that became saints; great women who did the work of God.

There were other saints like little Saint Tereasa, the little flower. The Little Flower was very soft, very gentle, and very melancholy. She was more introverted, more into God and the oneness of prayer. She liked to pray all day in the chapel. She liked helping the sick, but I did not want to be like Saint Tereasa the Little Flower.

I did not want to pray all day, and I did not want to help the Sisters in the infirmary. I did not want to walk softly, I wanted to be like the big Tereasa of Avala who went out and fought on the front for God. With that revelation, I began to sing more. I told Sister Veronica I would be like Tereasa of Avala. I would hold my head high and be proud for Jesus. I decided that I did not want humility; I wanted to be a leader. I felt good about taking leadership and I would use my leadership skills for the good of Jesus. I would put Jesus first in whatever I did; I wanted to be the best in whatever I did for him. Whatever challenge came my way, I was prepared to endure like a shining star.

Chapter Eleven: Fantasy to Fatality

As time went on, the convent became my home and my way of life. I received letters from my family and found that all the mail and packages, every single item that arrived in the convent, was censored. Letters to us would be read first by Novice Mistress or Mother Superior. When we received them, if we received them, they were opened. There were letters withheld; the person whose letter it was had to talk to either Novice Mistress or Mother Superior about them. Usually the letters withheld were those which expressed sadness or sorrow in the family. She would want to be the person who informed you of the sorrow or tragedy in the family. I always prayed that my mother or father would not die during this time because if there was a death in the family, it would have been very difficult for me to have taken the long journey to Florida. We were not permitted to travel if there was a death in the family. I would have had to make the decision to leave the convent for good in order to attend the funeral or be with my family. I prayed that I would not have to be faced with that decision.

We were taught that even our families were placed in God's care. So, our leaving the convent to be with our families meant very little since all of their consoling needs would be provided from on high. You must rid yourself of the things of the world and of the flesh, including the care of family members. You must pray for the loved ones who remained in the outside world even though you were set apart from them. This was a difficult task for me to do mentally, to separate myself from my family.

Yes, I was not apart of the outside world, but a part of me was still in that world. I used to say to myself, "how can I even rid myself of the world? How can I rid myself of that which they are asking me to do?" Part of me was in that world and was forever apart of that world. It would take some time for me to pass from the world that I was in to the new one I wanted to be in or what Sister Veronica wanted me to be in.

Gradually I began to change. I began to realize that I truly could be set apart from the world. You *could* leave loved ones in the world. During the three years I was in the novitiate, this is exactly what began to happen. I became more enrapt with God while performing my chores which embodied God. Even so, I never forgot to pray for my family. I always wanted my family to join me. I would not have minded if my mother, father, and sisters had come to see me. I even wanted them to come and live in the convent with me. I wanted the best for them, I thought that this was the best world I was living in and they were not apart of that world. I yearned for them to become apart of my world. I made them part of my world by placing them at the altar of God. I prayed for them everyday. I asked God to make them apart of the world I was enjoying. In doing that, I felt I had brought my entire family into the convent spiritually. During the period I was in the convent I never saw my family. I still pictured my sisters as little children even as they grew into adulthood.

Being a nun was something special to me. It was out of the ordinary as most aspects of my life had been. But then, I was always considered out of the ordinary. As an example, I was the only one in my family who had asthma as a child. Even later in my life, my experiences were special. I was accepted at the age of sixteen to the convent as a nun before completing high school—very much out of the ordinary. As I reflect on those early days in the convent I always considered myself only as a "partial nun." I could not wait until the first six months were over to become a novice. When that day came, I got the word in a very strange way. I actually thought I would never make it, many girls never made it to novice; they left during the first six months. After the first six months, they gave us another six-month probationary period. Others who didn't make it left within the probationary period. I thought that at some time they would call me in and tell me that I had to leave. When a girl was asked to leave, she always left at night, under the cover of darkness. I looked forward toward becoming a novice. I couldn't wait to become a Bride of Christ.

The Novice Mistress frequently called us in to tell us this or that about our progress. Had we improved in what we suggested or

144

were we holding back? I remember the last conversation I had with her; she tapped on my door and asked me to follow her to the other side of the house, past the kitchen in the direction of the refectory. We went toward the parlor, out of the cloister all together. When I heard the knock on the door, at first I thought, "Uh-oh, they must want *me* to leave the convent." Those who were asked to leave always received a knock at their door at night. I thought that it must have been my turn. We would not know that a girl had left until we arrived for breakfast the next morning or for prayers. At breakfast, the Novice Mistress would say, "Sister so and so was not fit for this life." We would then pray for the nun who had been asked leave.

They expected real changes in our lives and in our personalities. They watched how we cleaned, how we took orders, and what we said and did not say. They observed how we carried ourselves; how we cared for others. They monitored our sadness and happiness. They watched us when we got up in the morning and when we went to bed at night. I followed behind Sister Veronica and we went into the small parlor. She still had that smile that I remembered from the first night she talked to me in my cell. That great beautiful smile which said, "Praise be to Jesus and Mother Mary."

When we were seated, Sister Veronica spoke, "Now Sister, I want you to know that I expect more changes in you. I want you to know that you must make these changes, and it is very important that you make them."

Sister Veronica spoke softly as she explained what changes she wanted to see; changes in the way I worked with the Sisters in the host room. When I was told to wrap the host or to fold the paper a certain kind of way, I was to do it their way, not my own way. If I was told to place twenty hosts in a box, I was not to put any more or less in the box. If one of the Sisters asked for two veils to be ironed, I was not to complain about how very difficult it was, or about how after I washed the veils, I could not get the starch off of my hands. Sister Veronica said that I complained about setting the table and was very slow when setting the table and this gave her the feeling that I did not want to participate in setting the table. She said that when I was told to clean the priest's bathroom, I stayed in the bathroom half the day to avoid cleaning another one. Sister Veronica told me all of the things she was concerned about me changing.

"Yes, I want to make a change for Jesus," I said to her. "I will try to make these changes because I want to serve God."

"Alright, but you must *do* better and not just try to do better," replied Sister Veronica.

I went to my cell feeling sad. It seemed like she always chose the moment before bedtime to reprimand us. This meant that we had all these thoughts in our hearts and minds to ponder alone in our cells. There would be no one around to comfort or sympathize with us. There was no person I could talk with. It was after "grand silence" and not even whispering was allowed at this time. Only in a dire emergency were we allowed to talk and even that was in a whisper. I thought of how much I had given up to be at the convent.

"Does she know how I got here?" I asked myself. "How could she say these things to me? I have given so much to Jesus and here she is, telling me I had not given enough!"

My anger became outrage. I jumped out of bed, flew down the hall and banged on her door. Sister Veronica came to her door without her veil but with a white scarf.

"Yes sister, what seems to be the matter?" She whispered sweetly.

I responded without whispering, "I have to speak to you…now." I marched to the other side of the cloister and waited patiently for her with the lights on.

"I pondered what you said and I disagree with you. If that means that I have to leave the convent, I want to leave now. This experience will never stop me from loving and serving God. You don't have any control over my relationship with him. You are not God and I would never consider *you* in the seat of the judge."

I was adamant about being saintly and holy without the convent, I didn't need a nunnery for that. I lashed out at Sister Veronica throwing all of my mixed emotions in her direction. I had given up so much to prove my love of God and I was not going to let her take that away from me. I spoke to her in a very frank matter and I told her never to speak to me again about being proud because I would be proud for the rest of my life practicing the talent God gave me. I told her that I was not going to deny any talent God gave me and I would use it to the fullest. I would not try to be something I wasn't. I went on this vein until I began to unfold so much I really forgot where I was and who I was talking to. Surprisingly, I saw a warm smile at the corners of Sister Veronica's mouth.

"I don't want you to leave," she said. "You can become a saint. You can be perfect and I want you to stay."

I began to cry.

"Then why did you say all of those things to me? Why have you said so many mean things to me over the past months? Why do girls leave in the middle of the night?"

"It's different with you," she replied. Some girls don't have a vocation—a calling from God. Those that do, we must mold. We must groom them. It is my responsibility to groom you into perfection—to make you whole before God."

I explained to her that she discouraged me by telling me things I considered hurtful.

"What you said to me can never make me holy in the sight of God," I said.

"No that is not what I was trying to do to you" replied Sister Veronica.

Ignoring her protest I continued.

"I came here because it was something I wanted to do. I didn't get the idea from Catholic Church, school, or nuns. I am doing it of my own free-will…I love God."

Signaling the end of this confrontation, in the same soft voice she always spoke in, Sister Veronica said, "Now my child, go back to your cell and rest well, God be with you."

I left her without saying thank you, goodbye or goodnight. I had no more words for her. I was there and I knew what I had come there to do. I had made up my mind and I did not need her or anyone else to do it for me. After returning to my cell, I was wide awake. Lying on the bed, I asked God to give me grace and strength to go on, to be perfect in his sight and to give all I had to him. I prayed not to worry about what people may say or may not say. I asked God to give me the perfect prayer that would guide my life from that night hence forth. I remember becoming very calm as I reflected on St. Francis of Assisi, my favorite saint and finding oneness with myself that I had never experienced before. I drifted off to sleep very happy.

Chapter Twelve: Holy Bride in the Making

Several uneventful weeks followed until the day I was given a letter stating that I had been accepted into the convent as a Novice. I had been approved by Mother General and her council. It was approved that I would go on to become a Bride of Christ. I was in disbelief. This was a dream come true. All of the hard work and sacrifice contributed to my successful completion of the probationary period.

The Mother General and her council requested that I submit three names for myself now that I was an official Novice. They would choose from among the three names I submitted, but I would have no final say in the decision. Sometimes, they would give us one of our choices and at other times an entirely new name would be given to us. I made my three choices for a new name and one that I really liked, was the name Sister Noelita Marie because she had traveled the world.

I had the opportunity to meet Sister Noelita Marie when she came to the novitiate house to tell us about her journeys to the leper colonies, where she practiced medicine. She was a medical doctor and trained at a hospital in New York City. Sister Noelita spent time on missions and I had always dreamed of becoming a missionary and saving the world. She went where many would not go. She chose to go to the unwanted, exiled persons of any given society. I respected and admired her for that. I was curious about life in other parts of the world and world travel remains one of my most indulged activities.

I wanted to go far away to the missions in Africa. I had heard that Africa was one of the remote places where nuns could travel. I wanted to go to remote places despite the fact that we had teaching missions in New York City schools, along with teaching missions in the South and the Caribbean. As Sister Noelita Marie would tell us stories of the remote places she visited and worked, I empathized—I wanted to go to the remote villages like she had, in order to serve God. I was looking forward to being a missionary. I liked her name having the reference to Christ in Noelita. Noel means Little Christmas and Christmas comes from Christ. I wanted Christ in my name. I also wanted the Blessed Virgin's name in my name. Mary, Maria, or Marie would suffice. So Noelita Marie would be my new name. I decided on her name as my own.

In one of my classes at the convent, I learned about Jesus, the Blessed Virgin Mary, Joseph and the way of the cross. I found what each station stood for in the way of the cross, I learned the scriptures, to say my rosary and the crown to the Blesses Virgin. I also learned about preparation for a retreat. As a Novice, there was a lot I had learned in a short span of time.

The time had now come to prepare to become the Bride of Christ. I was given black fabric—many yards of it to make a habit. The habit is like a long flowing gown that nuns wear. It has a certain number of pleats. The number is prescribed by the order and everything is counted and measured to the "T." Everything stands for something; this was the particular style of their particular order. It was a trademark in a sense. The habit was a uniform and it had to be followed in its style and pattern. If there were supposed to be ten pleats, nine pleats or eleven pleats were unacceptable. We were taught how to make our own habits; if we didn't sew them or measure them correctly, we had to do it again until it was done correctly. We also learned how to cut out the skirt, vest, and sleeves, and how to put it all together. We learned how to make the double seam inside.

We learned how to create the habit by following precise directions. The long skirt was the first part.Then we learned to make the piece in the front that hides anything that is showing through the shirt called the scapula. The idea of it was to preserve the Sisters' modesty and to obscure the body form so that no bodily features were apparent under the habit.

The scapula hid any sexual appeal of the nun; someone might say that it helped hide a multitude of sins. After the scapula was made, we learned how to make our head bands, and how to starch them in Argo starch. Argo starch was before the era of spray starch. We mixed the powdery substance in a bowl of water until it foamed a clear liquid which almost solidified, making whatever was dipped in it extremely stiff. We dipped our things many times into the starch solution. Then we were taught to iron it so it stood up stiff on our heads. This was then placed between a coif, a piece of cloth cut out in the shape of the hand and stitched. Is this the correct spelling of this garment.

First, it was hemmed on a machine and then, it was placed around the face and adhered with a piece of gut on the neck. After that, it was pulled tight with pins in the back this way, your whole head, hair, and ears were covered up and finally, it was pulled up at the top and pinned very tightly so that it didn't have any wrinkles. It had to have a very neat and smooth look.

The head band was also white, which I mentioned earlier as having been stiff with starch. It fits on the coif down on the forehead, standing between the coif and the veil. The veil was white and we were taught to make it for ourselves by measuring shoulder to shoulder. Everything was measured for exactness in making a habit. Everything was customized for us. Our habits were the result of a lot of care and were made as perfectly as possible. Once the cloth had been cut, the various pieces were stitched so that there would be no loose or ragged edges on any of the pieces.

The veil was then placed on top of the band and a white hat pin went through the band. Any tailor would have envied our workmanship, especially in meeting the rigid measurement standards! All of the customizing details of a particular style of habit were part of the identity of the order. For example, when a nun saw me, she knew I was a Franciscan Nun. I would know another Handmaids Sister by recognizing the style and pattern of her habit. Our habits were discernable from all other habits. We learned how to dress ourselves; having to make our own habits, we naturally became very proficient seamstresses.

Sewing was a self-preservation skill in the convent. We also learned to cook, clean and take care of our every need. If any of us didn't have those skills when we arrived, we acquired them shortly after becoming part of convent life. We even learned how to make beads. We wore the crown—the *Franciscan Crown* it was called. The convent provided the chain and beads and taught us how to chain each bead. It hurt the hand and chaining the beads could even cut up the fingers, but, we learned how to make our own rosaries—the Franciscan Handmaids of Mary Beads.

We learned how to make the knots and there were three knots in our ropes so that we were able to wear them around our waists; the three knots were also associated with our faith. The rope had significance; it was a sign of poverty, charity, and obedience. The rope meant that we were Franciscan, meaning that we followed a particular saint, in this case, Saint Francis of Assissi. Different orders follow different saints. Saint Francis wore a rope around his waist, so all nuns that follow him wear ropes around their waists. Those were some of the lessons and preparation necessary to become a Bride of Christ.

Firstly, we were dressed in the ways of the world bride. We rehearsed in order to get prepared. Sister Bernadette whose specialty was grooming the future bride measured us for a bridal dress which had a train. We then went to the altar to marry Christ as a bride of the world in a wedding gown. We had flower girls too. The wedding was elaborate, vibrant, and beautiful. Everything was perfect. There is no union more perfect than that between a Sister and Christ. One might have practiced numerous times during a week for the perfect ceremony. We had to practice how to walk up the aisle and the songs that would be sung. We practiced how to do this and that, and how we would be changed at the altar. The little bridesmaids came to the convent to stay with us for a few days before the marriage was to take place. They had to practice and get accustomed to the ceremony so that it could be perfect.

The marriage was a very important ceremony and many Sisters from all over attended. Some nuns went into retreat before the wedding. The marriage took place in the spring after March and before Easter. The time of the year was symbolic and represented a renewal and birth. Every year we made at least two retreats. At that time of the year, nuns who taught school would be out for Easter recess. For eight days none of us were involved with anything worldly. The Sisters would come in from the missions and many others were granted absence from various assignments around the world to attend the retreats. The church informed us of our scheduled retreats. There were lots of nuns present for the marriage and seeing so many new faces was very exciting. Their presence rejuvenated the routine prayers and chores. Many of our visiting field sisters were older nuns. They were pros who tackled life outside of the convent while serving and loving God. We greatly anticipated their visits and realized it would take years of spiritual growth and grooming to be like them; it was something I looked forward to. This added another dimension to religious life, waiting for my turn to go out into the world.

Some of the nuns who came in for retreat would be making their final vows, while others would be making their temporary vows while others would be on retreat. A few were making jubilee celebrations. Jubilees were determined by the years devoted to being a nun and some celebrated golden jubilees, others celebrated silver jubilees. Golden jubilees marked more years as a nun. Some of the nuns just came in order to rest. In resting they renewed their spirits. It was a way to renew life, which was what the eight day retreat was all about, renewing life with God; to heighten the oneness and bring God back into full focus. It was not the material world we were about, it was the spiritual. During that time the house was different; there were more people in the place and more people moving around, but no one was heard speaking. It was still and silent in the convent.

We were lower key than usual and spent more time in our cells, alone. When the bells rung we performed whatever tasks the bell signified in the chapel or the refectory and through it all, we maintained a oneness with God through whispers and silence. We did not go outdoors for recreation. The time was used for reading, reflecting, praying, and resting. There was more time spent with the inner self. There were no external chores, no cleaning, cooking and the like, we did very little and most activities were abandoned during this time. It was my first retreat and I was very happy because it gave me a chance to read the books I had started and others I had long wanted to read. I didn't have to worry about listening for the bell ringing signaling other activities. It gave me more time to myself. It gave me more time to rest. No one cared what you did during this time. I enjoyed being by myself if only to sit in my room and think. I could sleep for an extra hour or spend the whole morning in my cell undisturbed. I enjoyed that time very much.

I have vivid memories of the night before the Bride of Christ ceremony. I wanted to have everything perfect. My habit was laid out for me in the chair. The bib was laid out; it was also starched and ironed. The snappers were sewn on properly and my shoes were shined to a mirror finish. My stockings were laid out for me and my veil was starched and ironed. Everything we were to wear the next morning was prepared and visible. This was the ultimate; it was the marriage to Christ. From the first moment I possessed my habit lying on the bed, to the bridal gown that hung on the door of the closet; the veil and the making of the flowers which were going to form a wreath for my hair, all was waiting for me for the next morning. I anticipated the next morning. I went to Morning Prayer as a postulate but I said to myself, "soon I will be a Novice! I will take off all of this black that I brought with me and leave it behind."

This would be the first time the convent gave me clothes. I would change from the clothes I brought from the south to those given to me at the convent. After Morning Prayers, there was no mass because the main mass was going to be the ceremony. The prayers were shorter in the morning. Then we ate breakfast during which we heard, "Dominus Nobisum." Everyone responded with, "Deo Gracius" which brought us out of the eight days of silence. There was buzzing and whispering. The sound of Sisters were heard whom I never heard speak before. We mingled with the professional Sisters; it was not allowed when we were in training. This was the first time that we were able to see them and laugh with them. Both Novices and Superiors were talking with one another; never before had I heard all of this noise. I saw sisters who were old friends embrace; kiss each other on the cheek, and say, "Praise be to Jesus of Mary Sister." It was a happy scene. The professional Sisters brought another kind of spirit into the novitiate house. The Sisters would say to us that they were looking forward to our becoming Novice Sisters and that they would be present for the ceremony. It was all very exciting and I couldn't wait. These are the kinds of greetings I received. The professional Sisters let us know that they were there for us. The meetings added a great spirituality to becoming a nun.

It was close to the time for us to return to our cells and I heard the swooshing of habits and the sounds of beads making the air even tenser with excitement. The slow gait of an older Sister, the quick steps of a younger Sister; the sounds of the moving bodies added to the spiritual energy floating around the convent. Exciting things were happening in our lives; I was going to become a Bride of Christ and all the Sisters would be watching. I was hoping that my family received the letter informing them of my marriage so that they could be in attendance spiritually. I also hoped Sister Laura received my letter, I couldn't wait! I wasn't certain that my folks knew about the blessed event but I went back to my room overwhelmed with joy anyway. This was a big day in my life even if my family was not there as in the traditional wedding ceremonies.

I was sitting in my room and all of a sudden there was a knock on the door. It was the Sister who had come to help me get dressed. Sister Bernadette was in charge. I'll never forget it. She was in charge of the band of three. She wanted everything to be perfect. One of the other Novices came into my room to help me dress. There was nothing I could forget. Everything I put on was brand new—undershirt, t-shirt, and slip. I came to the convent with a dowry and these things were apart of it. If I remember correctly, my dowry cost $200, and purchased all the new things I needed for my wedding. The other clothes in the dowry were to last for a year. We were supplied with a list of how many towels, sheets, pillow cases, and the like we would need for the year. We even supplied our own table wear and sanitary napkins. On this special day, the Sister you had come to help you dress would style your hair any way you wanted. Candy curls, straight, or any style desired. My hair had grown so it was touched up a bit and curled.

The first thing the Novice did to help was getting me into my white stockings. She then helped me into my high heel shoes and slipped my beautiful flowing gown on. This was the bride of the world. Whatever the latest bridal fashion was, we wore. Our dresses had long trains. This was a first class wedding all the way—there was nothing skimpy about it.

Sister Bernadette, who was responsible for the outcome of the wedding, had impeccable taste and chose the best for Christ's Bride; this Sister had a natural talent for dressing women. She would have made a good personal shopper in the outside world. We took vows to give God the best of what was in us, therefore the Sister who came to dress us and the ceremony itself lacked nothing. The gown was made of the best laces, the finest silk and the best possible ornamentation. The quality of the ceremony was to reflect a quality of God. There was a serious commitment to perfection and quality. Vogue Magazine would have reported nothing less. That's the way it was, nothing was done half-heartedly. If anything was out of place Sister Bernadette would devote hours to bringing it to a stage of perfection. This attentiveness she applied to all aspects of the wedding. The gown was a sample of perfection. The veil was a work of art. My flower girl was a vision of loveliness. I was given a bouquet of flowers and flowers for the flower girl. At the last minute Sister Bernadette came rushing to see if everything was perfect and that we were fully fluffed out.

Everyone in the chapel had on their best garments. There was perfect uniformity in the chapel. The entire affair was a class act.

It was well organized and invitations went out to family members and whomever else you wanted to receive one. The convent officials also invited people. I did not see my family coming to this ceremony because the event was so short and they were so far away. I was not even sure if that had received my announcements in time since it was rather late when I sent them out. When I left home I told my family that I would never see them again, so they probably didn't recognize the announcement as an invitation to attend the ceremony. Even though my family wasn't there, most of the people who attended I recognized. I had seen many of the nuns before and they treated me like family.

Chapter Thirteen: The Marriage to Jesus

The chapel was crowded. The brides were lined up outside and we could hear all the activities in the chapel in preparation for us. We had a gorgeous day; the Sun shone in all its glory, emanating brightly as it was suspended in a cloudless blue sky. The warmth of the Sun heightened the aroma of the flowers of the surrounding gardens and their sweet smells wafted through the chapel carried by the light breeze. Everyone had been seated in the chapel when the bell rang and the future brides were led closer to the chapel door. Now, the ceremony was ready to begin.

Candles were lit and the singing started. The voices singing in unison was extraordinarily exquisite. It sounded like God had sent some of his angels down for this blessed event. It was like the singing of the heavenly host; angels singing sweet harmony in glorification of God like nothing I had ever heard before; it was truly awesome. The voices were crystalline and pure; I felt I could have stated there forever just listening. The Sisters were well trained in the art of singing for God and they were devoted to giving their best. All the beautiful sounds mixed and harmonized sweetly in the small space. There were sounds coming into the chapel from outside. You could hear the birds singing mixed with the soft rumble of the nearby surf, enhancing the beauty and spiritualism of the ceremony. It was celestial! Even I, the little songbird who had grown up with the superb singing of Mahalia Jackson, Sam Cooke and the Five Blind Boys, was still moved by what I heard. Marian Anderson was my role model for singing. I was exposed to and appreciated wonderful singing.

So there I stood, preparing to marry Christ. My head was held up high. I was enveloped on all sides by the melodic singing as I moved down the aisle. I was the youngest and therefore, the last bride in line. Sister Rita was first since she was the oldest, then Sister Sherry, and finally, it was time for me to go down the aisle with my flower girl. I felt like as if I was on cloud nine, floating way above the ground to the altar. I was going to meet the bridegroom. At the altar I knelt. Mass was being held and prayers were being said. The ceremony was before us. The Bishop, Monsignor and the Mother General were there. The clothes we had made were lying in the chairs waiting to be blessed and holy water sprinkled on them. Incense was blown on the new clothes.

After the clothes had been blessed, they were given to us with a prayer. With the Sisters singing angelically, we took the clothes and left the chapel. Right on our heels were the Sisters responsible for undressing us and helping with our new clothes—our new way of life. This was a solemn time; exciting while being very holy, and very special.

We moved through the cloister back towards our cells to take off the wedding gowns and put on our habits and veils before returning to the altar. At this point, we no longer wore the garments of the world and have now put on the robe of God. With that change we also rid ourselves of the ways of the world and accepted the ways of God. In some orders the nun's hair was cut, but not in ours. A piece of hair is cut off to symbolize discarding vanity. Some orders felt that giving up one's hair was giving up a treasured symbol of physical beauty in the outside world. At the altar our black veils were placed on us—the Franciscan Crown. We were then given our prayer books, our Matins and Lords; our vespers. The vespers was the book containing all of the prayers we needed to have. With the prayer books we were armed with God's word; we were also given crucifixes.

The crucifix is symbolic of the suffering, the penance and tribulations we were expected to endure for the good of Christ. Christ died for all of us and this symbolizes that our lives should be ones of penance, suffering and modification of life; perseverance, and as testament to faith in Christ during it all. During the time of suffering and joy, we were to remember that Christ paved the way for us to live a life of holiness. Whatever we did, we could press on with confidence, determination, and the knowledge that Christ is the way, the truth and the life. The black veil was pinned in a way as to be held by a white wreath which was placed over the veil. This symbolized that we were the Brides of Christ and would dedicate our lives to attaining holiness and perfection spiritually. We pulled off the old and donned ourselves with the new. As of that day we had whole new lives. We forgot about the past; we were new women on the new track of life.

"Do you take off the old and put on the new?" we were asked.

"I do," we responded.

I was overwhelmed. I wanted everybody to know that I loved God. "I do" meant something very special to me. Taking our vows also meant that we would study the ways of Christ. We vowed to take on chastity, a life without sex, poverty and obedience. We were to learn what we had to do to live perfectly; we had to get to know the groom. The next two years would be a very, very serious period in our lives. We were going to learn everything about the life of Christ and how his life became our lives. We had to learn how to embody and enrapture ourselves in Christ. How does one become one with Christ? It was not just about getting married; any good marriage requires work. I had to make a commitment which was only symbolized by the ceremony. The commitment was not fulfilled there. How to work and strive toward that goal was the question which was to be contemplated everyday. In the two years that followed, our lives were to be holy, perfect and prayerful.

The bridegroom had not met the bride yet, the irony of it all. We claimed to have taken off the old ways as a bride but, Christ said,

"You just came to me, you are not ready to see me." It's like courting, you find the man you love; you primp and dress up for him and place yourself at his feet, but you have not walked the last mile yet. There is preparation before you walk the last mile. You are still waiting for the groom to come to you. You still have your virginity and have not slept with him; the oneness is yet to come. This is what it was like for the Novice. The Novice was into a serious and profound seeking of truth of self and of the Lord. She wanted to prepare herself beautifully and she waited for him to fully receive her.

Chapter Fourteen: Excloistration

If you think the nun experience is a unique sojourn, the ex-nun experience is a sojourn of a bolder type. I had not been out of the convent a month when I found myself in Marcus Garvey Park. I saw a group of junkies standing around the park. I did not see any that I knew in particular but apparently, one of them knew me and shouted, "Hey Sister, where are your nun clothes?!" I approached him and told him what I had done. He was so surprised he couldn't resist the opportunity of punning and my expense.

"She kicked the habit and never looked so good!" Bobby exclaimed loudly.

The other junkies who heard the last part of what he said came rushing over to look at me. They inspected my arms for track marks and just marveled about how well I looked since I had kicked the habit.

"Where is Bumpy I can't find my protection as I run the streets of Harlem?" I said, "We don't know" The junkies replied. "I'm going to get Bumpy on you all." I said with a smile and a high five.

Actually, at that time, I had not completely kicked the habit. As a rule, a nun takes vows and does not get rid of them easily. I was in a period called "excloistration" a trial period away from the convent. This period was in consideration of the nuns who were just a bit claustrophobic in the convent and who opted to return to the convent after discovering where they belonged in life.

For some Sisters, a short time away from the convent brought them face to face with their reality. The convent and the adherence to the rituals of the money were the satisfactory alternatives and not the outside world. So, at that time I was still a nun in street clothing, so to speak. I figured at the time that I had to get out of my system whatever it was emotionally that caused me to leave the Covent. I needed to explore a number of facts of life while I was free to do so I if I decided I wanted to return to the Covent after this period. Put another way, I would be better able to decide to go back or not when I had experienced some other alternative lifestyles and points of view.

In New York City, a point of view is often related to geography. A restaurant on Park Avenue in the fifties is surround by a different culture than a restaurant on 42nd street. A Sutton place resident perceives differently than a resident of Spanish Harlem. Their behaviors may not be dissimilar but their points of view will be. The point of view I adopted was that I had to cram a lifetime of experiences into one year. Could it be done? Would it take longer than a year? Would I abandon that quest after a year and return to the convent? What unknown possibilities would I be incubating so blindly? I wondered. Was it naïve of me to be homeless with very little money? God I hoped not. But, it was clear to me that once the questions raised themselves there was no way I could turn my back on them. Once I asked those questions, they became issues in my life. The resolution of them held the promise of a greater self understanding.

The successful resolution of these issues led to advancement; failure led to more distress. The more light shined on the issues the greater the personal rewards. In New York City there were a lot of lights, the city lights. They turned on in my mind and the points of view blended together to create behavior. One's behavior in the city, in turn created more lights and points of view. I got different points of view about life in and out of the convent by a simple change in geography. That fact alone took me to the streets. The streets of New York City were paths to transformations. They connected experiences and being in the streets gave me a lot of time to think.

By the time I started walking along 42nd street, the issues in my life had already been changed. During these times I thought more about what happened after dark. Would innocent curiosity tarnish a jaded self survival point of view? Would my feelings of universal goodwill change into a conniving ulterior self presentation? I hated those moments when I began to see others as possible meal or a caretaker for me until the next day without compromising my body. It was not easy.

My meals were satisfying. Dining in style was never a problem. There were many fancy restaurants in New York City with such grace and style that it was out of the question to prosecute the occasional lout who could not pay her bill. I would announce to the

manager that indeed I could not pay my bill because of a sudden
reversal of my finances but I would be more than happy to was
dishes or serve tables to compensate for the cost of my meals. They
insisted that the whole matter would be forgotten if I could promptly
leave and made sure I never showed my face in their establishments
again. But that was then. I am sure that now the same place would
prosecute to the hilt anyone who pulled that stunt these days,
pinched high class or not.

I do not recommend that style of dinning to anyone. I asked
God to forgive the misrepresentation of nuns; I also thanked him for
the excellent food. If anyone were to attempt what I did, I reiterate
that I don't recommend it, but if anyone did, pick a classy place like
the Plaza, the Waldorf, or the Palace. They may not have the pinch
other places have. They are places of grace and they may let you
leave peacefully rather than handcuffed. Besides, they have better
food!

I began to miss the convent; the meals on time and the quiet
comfort of my room. I recalled fondly that exciting time when
Mother Teresa of Calcutta lived with us in our convent. I recalled
how exotic their cuisine was and the strange aromas that wafted

through the hallways. It is funny how hunger changes one's appetite. At such periods I longed for the exotic Indian cooking that I was not very fond of. The convent I mused was about sharing. We shared money, points of view and duties. How discomforting it is to have to survive alone. When the strong survive, the "me versus "you" issue becomes apparent in the competitive survival style. Some have it easy, others have more difficulties. The losers in the struggle to survive whom I identify as those who use immoral or unethical strategies have no such luck as those who lives were handed to them on a silver platter. I don't believe we should look down upon the less fortunate because the difference between being better or worse off may have just been an accident.

When I got a job, I satisfied the ethical and moral question of survival. I worked for about a month at J.C. Penny. I also worked for a relief organization during the Nigerian civil war. At that job, people I came across thought I was from Africa. In our relief work, we tried to raise money and collect food for the Biafrans affected by the war in Nigeria. I was able to get the management of J.C. Penny to listen to me and sponsor the drive for the Biafrans. I also worked briefly at Chemical Bank on Park Avenue near Grand Central Station.

Later, I worked at a UNICEF card store; a box factory, and a stocking factory.

After I started my working life, living at the Adam Clayton Powell Residence for Women, I moved into my own apartment after a few months. During this time I maintained myself with temporary jobs. Gradually, I bought clothes, earrings and small necessities; I was learning how to dress. It was at this time that I was given a scholarship to attend the Barbizon School of Modeling where I learned about daytime and evening wear. I learned about clothes for dining and about make-ups.

The modeling classes were very exciting. They prepared me for my training as a hand model. My role was to display jewelry because I was thought to have lovely hands. I was a runway model; I was told I had an elegant back and I carried garments well. During that period, I learned a lot about fashion, modeling beauty and walking properly. Through associates, a beneficiary, Louise, found me and was responsible for my scholarship to Barbizon. I also took some courses in modern dance; Percy Boyd and Pearl Promise worked with me during that time. They thought I was capable of having a professional career in modeling and dancing. Percy Boyd was responsible for my getting a scholarship to Harkness Ballet. When they heard that I had come out of a convent they could not believe it. They were in awe at the fact that I had no previous dancing experience. The activities were good outlets for me and a good means for moving through society. The classes kept me quite busy during my year out of the convent. I also joined a health spa where I was able to meet many people and stay in shape.

Before I realized it, the year of excloistration was over. I had to make a decision to return to the convent or remain out of it. I got a letter from the convent to that effect. I called the Mother Superior and informed her that I would not return to the convent, I was making a complete adjustment to the outside world. I received another letter lifting me of my vows to the Franciscan Handmaids of the Most Pure Heart Mary. When the letter came I removed my wedding band and any traces of convent affiliation. This included the crucifix I wore around the neck. These were artifacts of my past which I removed as a symbol of the beginning of my new life. I remember I was particularly lonely at that time.

I had the burden of settling those issues of my life, all alone. The next day I called Denise, Sandra, the rest of my friends and people who knew me and my connection with the convent and informed them that I had officially cut off my ties with the church. I was now truly a woman of the world and no longer Sister Noelita Marie. I especially called all the men I knew to let them know that I was now a woman. These were men I liked and that was my way of telling them that I was available but they failed to comprehend what I was doing. It later dawned on me that all the men I had known when I was a nun still regarded me as one. When I invited them to come over to my place, they would not come. So now, I had to go out of my way to make friends with men who did not know me as a nun.

Chapter Fifteen: Birth of a New Future

I did not start out being social climber. Social climbing is a necessity I learned after I left the convent. As I said earlier, the streets of New York City taught me that all people were equal in the sight of God. I saw no reason why where a person lived determined how they treated another person. It was true that location was an important issue to most New Yorkers. After all, Park Avenue was not Chinatown. I was a bit naïve on that matter perhaps.

I did not need that naivety to know early in life that people judged you by appearance. It was a game people played. If you bought your clothes at Lord and Taylor's and people respected you. Arriving at a reception in a long limousine and rebuke those who might doubt your worth. I found it all a bit tiring. It must be destructive to the human spirit. Look at the numbers of human discards who failed to move up the social ladder or who became victims of the process.

On the one hand, the fact of appearance was normal here. Anyone who attempted to change that fact was up against a system that delighted in superficiality. On the other hand, there was no way out. We were all captives of a reprobable society we held so dear. Even at that time, I saw my 42nd street moral illumination undergo some changes. I still had the ethical insight which I thought was the only way out, but the pressure to conform to the New York City game was too great for me to ignore. I had three choices leave town, return to the streets, or play the game to win.

I began thinking about the work I would do in my life when it occurred to me that the work I would do would probably be an extension of the work I performed as a nun. The nursery school we nuns operated taught me the importance of reaching the children long before they had potential problems with education, unemployment, or substance abuse. Children were a delight to me. They responded warmly to kindness. As far as I was concerned there was not enough being done for them. For the following several decades, I developed advocacy and direct services for children and the youth. I was not sure how social climbing would figure into my decision, but I did not dismiss it as a possible strategy.

Success in life when, and if it comes, is never an accident. Despite my inexperience in succeeding in the outside world, I give myself a lot of credit for planning comprehensively. To anyone who wants to pursue success in life I say, plan, plan, plan, and plan some more. When planning, one must consider the context of time and space; the long and short term goals, remembering that social climbing is a strategy and not the end; keeping a sharp eye on needs and limitations. Remember at all times to stay focused and keep your soul in the process; don't lose it. But, all is easier said than done. Armed with the insights from the streets, and a little perception of how the game was played, I sought to reconcile my ambitions and limitations with the realities of the city so called New York City.

The world always has you do one thing when you want to do another. When the world can give you what you want, the temptation to pay with your soul is forever present. I planned my social climbing for the survival of my soul. Who would think of the desire to help children receive educations would be fraught with the, "it's not what you know, but who you know." That was the state of affairs that I discovered for myself. I guess that too was part of the reality. I knew that if I were ever to make any contribution to education for children, it was my responsibility to accept all these realities, get out in the jungle, and build up the needed resources. I learned to win the game starting with geographical game. I started out in Washington Square Park. Harlem was still in my mind but my plan called for a much broader based multi-ethnic approach, and for more money than Harlem had. Washington Square Park was similar and dissimilar to Marcus Garvey Park. They were both green respites from the concrete canyons; a place to observe. The biggest difference was that now I was in contact with students from New York University.

I must have gotten a lot attention from the NYU students who observed me organizing a multiracial group of children for recreation. Some students from the university volunteered to become my companions and assistants. They questioned what I was doing and why, where I came from, and where I was going. Their innocent desire to help me was refreshing compared to the politics I confronted later. With the assistance of the students from NYU, I planned the concept of multiethnic education as an answer to New York City's geographical isolation of various communities. I planned the appearance of what I was looking for, a status address and of course New York University's unquestionable integrity.

Before long, the student's leader Bob Satiago, who "discovered" me in Washington Park, petitioned the University to "take me in." I received a lot of assistance from NYU. They gave me an office, the use of some their services and a little cash to support the work with the youth in the park. They helped me shape the plan that would later become the New Future Foundation (NFF), and gave me advice as to how to move into the system. Knowing how important appearances were, I was determined to satisfy that requirement by moving to 24th street Fifth Avenue, a very impressive address. By the time I had moved to my new address, NYU gave me a salary. They also gave me credibility and a good reference. In my analysis I got my start at NYU. It was a start but by no means was it an end.

I became a social climber for the good of the children and the programs I had in mind. When my period of funding was about to end, I learned from the people at the university how programs such as mine were funded by the City. That must have been my first exposure to altruistic sounding names such as the Children's Aid Society, The Greater New York Fund and, the New York City Mission Society. I liked the sounds of the names and they suggest who would be sympathetic with what I was doing. My enthusiasm became tarnished with the fear of politics that any encounter with these institutions might require. I decided to play the game and approach the possible sources of funds with a positive mind.

By the time I met Ms. Beaulah Watson of the Greater New York Fund, I had a good reputation. I had a good start on my track record that was needed to get support. In addition, Dave Barry of the New York City Mission Society agreed to be my fiscal agent because I, by myself, would not satisfy the accounting requirements needed to be funded directly. Sitting in Ms. Watson's office on that day, I knew exactly what I would say for the good of the program I was envisioning and, for the children who would be the beneficiaries. Our talk together had centered on my experience as a nun, the program I started at Washington Square Park, and my association with New York University. She questioned me about the amount of money such a program would cost, and the disposition the fund would take regarding grass roots community education projects. With my qualification already discussed and my need justified, I looked into her eyes with great profoundness.

"Give me the $9,000 I need to build the program and the next time I come to you I would have turned it into $100,000." I continued trying my best to convince her that she would reap the benefits of my plan. "Trust me with your money, it will be a small risk and you will never regret it."

I received every penny I requested. With that victory I became very confident. It is funny how money from some institutions was like an anointing. It was a certification that I was acceptable, but more than that, I was certain that I was on my way up. Here I was an ex-nun, residing on 24th and Fifth Avenue, and the recipient of public funds. That meant I could be trusted, it meant that I could build a multi=ethnic program.

The Fifth Avenue Hotel was the setting for the middle of this life story. I was the setting in which a major change in my circumstance and assumptions about life were wrought. The hotel was an outstanding place to live, work, and move up in life. Stevie Wonder was one of my neighbors and we had dinner together in my apartment in his honor. Some people just accepted me for being in their same social milieu. I had countless other famous neighbors including David Dubinsky, David Summerson, and Morris Ernst. I discovered that money, or the appearance of money, brought money. Nothing succeeded more than success; as the old saying goes, "them that got is them that gets." The old saying did not survive for nothing and sadly I discovered that it was all true.

Living at the Fifth Avenue Hotel was part and parcel of my whole fortune. I was a good person; I could be trusted for the simple and universal values I represented. That perception followed me even after I left the convent. People at the hotel who came know me shared their friends and knowledge with me not only because I shared their points of view but because we lived at the same address and were of equal status. Also, anyone dedicated about recreation for children was good; I would not harm anyone. With these assumptions made about me, my social climbing began to flower.

Rich men, powerful industrialists, usually white, were my escorts. What was that something I possessed which these men enjoyed to share? Was it compassion for the homely young black girl who perused an impossible dream so naïvely? Or, was it the promise that I could bring some man honor and glory as the righteous mother of his children? Was it just the loyalty and goodness of the woman who was a nun? I believe I t was all of these things combined. Looking back, I sometimes wonder if I did the right thing.

Chapter Sixteen: Of Men, Love, and Sex

On the question of matrimony, I hedged. On the question of sex, I did not need to respond. Most of the men I ran across did not want my body right away. Most of them hedged on the matter. Seeing, as I was homely, they figured that sex did not need to be rushed into. I simply told them that building an institution for children was my main goal, and that would require most of my time and focus for some time to come. It was interesting to see how people differ in their orientation to the world; I would have thought that most people would smile upon the chance to see children and

the underprivileged get a better chance in life. I discovered that was
not always true.

Burt, a man who made it big by working hard, disciplining
himself, and sacrificing a lot along the way, did not see the value in
helping others. He felt that as his wife, I might use his money for
those who would not help themselves. These men might have liked
me for the values these pursuits suggest, but they didn't want me to
pursue these goals after we were married. I had a choice in my
strategy to success in life; take the marriage route, with its sacrifices in
terms on my interests, or risk doing it my way or by myself. I was
lucky I did not have to make that choice. If you hedge just for a
moment, many male egos will not stand for it. "It's as good as saying
"no." Some would see any further communication from me as using
their interest in me, as a tool to get what I wanted. Most would not
allow their vulnerability to be seen any longer and that is when they
would fade from my life. However, that is the end of the courting
story; the beginning was much more exciting. As I began to put my
comprehensive plans to work, I became a human-interest story.

An ex-nun who organized a multi-ethnic recreational
program was something of a novelty. Rich white people interpret

that passion as high character, as did other ethnic groups. I was looked up to by all segments of society. There was nothing I pursued that could be denied. The good life resided a doorstep away and came seeking me over the telephone lines. I observed life from the private boxes of Lincoln Center as guest of my friends. I traveled the streets of New York City with a different point of view, behind the tinted windows of a stretch limousine with a white chauffeur. I became the confidant of the wealthy. That within itself was interesting. From that experience, I learned never to judge people by appearances. Anyone would think that in New York City, those who had money and had overcome the biggest challenge of the city's high cost would not have difficulties. However, some problems do not discriminate. The rich and the powerful also had their set of everyday woes. Stories of distrust, adultery, homosexuality causing disinheritance, social anxiety involving paranoia over monetary issues were just a few of the issues that I came across. I could certainly see why the rich men who hinted at marrying me backed down. They probably thought I would take their money and give it to who they believed to be the undeserved. It may sound unfair, but money was the root of all of their problems.

While they may have hinted at marriage with me, it was because they believed we shared the same social milieu. Truth be told, I had no money and shared the culture of poverty with those they looked down upon which was part of the reason why I never married a rich man. They observed me as a woman who loved the poor and downtrodden, a basic value that I could not deny despite my Fifth Avenue surroundings. Fifth Avenue or not, I was a bag lady at heart. The Fifth Avenue address was part of the strategy I pursued to win acceptance for my New Future Foundation program. I never saw it for anything else. As a person with basic needs, I never regarded the trappings of 24 Fifth Avenue as anything other than a lot of bricks put together on a particular site, which society had agreed was better than another place. That was all it was and all it could ever become. In the end I had reason to doubt whether it was even that much. But that's another part of the story yet to be told after my upward mobility was transformed; sending me back to Harlem penniless, homeless, and with a new addition, my daughter Ini Chinwa, profoundly mentally, and physically handicapped.

My first experience in courting was with an ex-priest. I thought because he was an ex-priest he would understand. He was from Spain, and very handsome. I invited him over for dinner at my place and made a very cozy, candlelit dinner for both of us. Here we were, both out of the church seeking to live life as secular people. Throughout the whole evening, I kept calling him "Father" by mistake, which didn't help in my attempt to seduce him. I knew for sure that he would not let me sit on his lap or anything like that, so, I contented myself with listening to music with him during his visit. He kissed me on the cheek and I kissed him on the cheek as well, but that was the extent of our intimacy. He left soon afterwards and from then on, we were just friends.

One day, I went to go pay some bills. I was thinking about my state of affairs with the opposite sex and concluded that a relationship would probably come naturally, one day; I just had to wait fro the right time. While on the line at Con Edison, a nice man smiled and asked if I would like to skip him in line. His name was Michael and he was West Indian. As we were talking, Michael told me that I was very pretty and I thanked him for the compliment. Then, he asked me for my number and I gave it to him and told him to give me a call later that night. Later that evening, the telephone rang. I was excited because I was expecting Michael to be on the other end of the line.

"Hi, do you remember me from the Con Edison office? My name is Michael."

"Of course I remember you."

"Are you having dinner?" Michael Asked.

"Well, I didn't start cooking yet but, would you like to join me for dinner?" I responded. "Sure," he said. "I would love to."

Chapter Seventeen: Plucking the Apple

It all happened accidentally. One night I was on the telephone and dialed the wrong number. I reached an answering service. It gave me a message that Dr. Magin called. So I repeated the name given to me and tried to place a face with the name. I said to myself a doctor is what I needed so I took the number and called. The doctor answered.

"Dr. Magin here."

"Dr. Magin?" I said.

"Yes" he responded.

"You have a very charming voice." I said.

"And so do you."

"Thank You." I said.

"Do you like chicken?" asked Dr. Magin.

"I love chicken."

"Would you like to have some chicken with me?"

"Yes, I would."

"Well," he began, "may I pick you up and take you out to dinner?"

I paused. "You're kidding, are you serious?"

"Yes, very" he replied.

"Well…what time will you be coming for me?"

"That depends on where you live."

I told him my name and address and he said that he would be there in forty-five minutes to an hour. I told him that I would get ready.

Sure enough, my bell rang after forty-five minutes. I went downstairs, dressed and perfumed. The brother came out of his car and there he was, a beautiful black man. I couldn't believe it, and to top it all off he drove a Mercedes Benz! So, we headed to a restaurant that was open late being that it was around 11:30 P.M. After, our dinner he brought me back home. We talked about what I was into and what I did with my time. He told me he was a psychoanalyst and that he had a practice in the Village. I told him I would like to talk to him about something and asked if he would call me the next day. He said that he would and kissed me on the forehead telling me to sleep well. The next night, he called me like he promised around eight o'clock.

"What are you doing?" he asked.

"I'm just relaxing."

"Do you want someone to relax with?"

"I wouldn't mind if that someone is you."

"Then I guess I'll see you later."

That night, when Dr. Magin arrived, I was happy. I found myself liking him a lot, he was a charmer. He had class and sophistication, and there was no doubt I was attracted to him. I told him that there was something that I wanted to talk to him about that was important in my life. He asked what it was and I told him that I had been a nun for ten years; I had left the convent a year ago. I had not had a relationship with a man and didn't know what to do in one since I had been rejected before. Men kept me as a sister and that was all.

"I want a man that will go to bed with me." I said.

"That's, a tall order you're placing on a man."

"Yeah, but it seems like men are afraid of sharing that with me, they keep running away."

"Well men will do that when a woman says that she wants to bed them."

"So what should I do?" I asked.

"How about I spend some more time with you and we talk about it?"

"I hope that you're not like the rest, they said the same thing you know."

"I'll call you tomorrow." He said.

He called the next day to tell me how sweet he found me to be. He told me not to worry and that I would make the adjustment in time, and that men would care for me. That really boosted my ego. We started speaking more often. There were times when I would call him four times in a night. We spent more time together and I enjoyed every minute of it.

I finally told him that I wanted him to make love to me. He agreed. He told me that it would take time and that there were so many things that went on before one made love. This was the talk I heard before when guys weren't interested. But this was different; he actually planned out when we would have our big night. I was so excited I didn't know what to do and so I called my father. I told him that I had found a man to make love to me and this of course shocked him. He told me that he was coming to New York City right away and sure enough, the next day, I found him lounging in my apartment when I got home.

When Dr. Magin arrived later that night I didn't tell him my father was going to be visiting for the weekend. I also did not tell him that my father would be sleeping in the bedroom. Leon and I were restricted to the living room where he wanted to make love. We didn't actually make love though. We caressed each others bodies and kissed each other. I thought I was supposed feel like I wanted to jump up and down and scream, but I didn't feel like it was anything special. I told Leon that what we did, did not feel the same way people described it. He told me it would take time and that this was something that we would work on.

The next day I told my father about the experience and I told him that I didn't like it. My father shared his first experience with me. He told me how awkward it was even after he had more experience with it.

"It never stops feeling a little awkward," said my father. "It's important to have only one partner that you have a special bond with. That eliminates some of the awkwardness."

"Well, I don't have strong feelings for Leon; I just want someone to make love to me."

"Delois, sex is not something a person just decides to do. You have to trust the person that you wish to be intimate with."

"I like Leon but, I don't think I fully trust him yet. I don't know…it's just so confusing!"

"Listen sweetie, there is a man out there for you. It may be Leon but it may not be. Just do not rush anything."

My father seemed to understand what I was going through. I was glad that I was able to express my feelings to him. He stayed with me for a few more days and then he returned to Ft. Lauderdale.

Leon called me about two weeks later and asked me if I wanted to try it again and I said I would. When we started, he asked me the same dumb questions repeatedly. He touched my breasts and asked how it felt. He touched my vagina, and my legs and my toes and asked again, how it felt. I said to him, "Oh, that's nice," but it really didn't feel that way. Then, he wanted me to touch his body, and following his lead, I asked him how it felt when I touched him. He started oohing and aahing exclaiming how great it felt. I was tickled by this; he grabbed me hugging me gently, and rubbing my back. After we had finished caressing each other's bodies, he said he had to leave. This went on for months. He would come over we would kiss and caress and then he would leave. But, I began to know what to expect and became familiar with his body as he did with mine.

One time when Leon came over, he said that he wanted to try something different. He took out a prophylactic and told me what it was. I'll never forget it, it was in a blue wrapper. We talked about it, and I learned it was lambskin. He said that it was already lubricated. He said that we was going to hug and kiss me and insert his penis into my vagina for the first time. He told me to let him know how it felt each step of the way. If I felt uncomfortable I was to let him know right away.

"The last thing I want to do is hurt you Delois" he said.

He started kissing me and caressed my naked body. When he started to insert his penis, I told him that I felt pain. He was gentle and did not force his way. After another attempt at which I felt more pain, he decided it would be better to withdraw and try it again another time. The next day, I did not call at all. He thought that it was strange because up until that point, I called him everyday. He called me later that day and asked me what was wrong. He said that it was not like me not to call him.

"What's the matter Delois? I got no messages on my answering service."

"I didn't feel like calling you."

I did not want to talk to him at all I was still trying to figure out my own feelings. When he called later that evening, I burst into tears. It seemed as if as soon as I hung up the phone, Leon was knocking on my door. We sat down and talked. I told him about my sentiments concerning sex; it was quickly vanishing as an object of my curiosity. I no longer felt the same motivation towards it. I told him that I didn't like what I was doing and it did not seem to make much of a difference in my life. He said that he didn't want me to feel that way about a new experience in my life nor about wanting to be close to a man. He thought that it was very important not to shy away from an experience, which did not develop fully. I was in my pajamas and he hugged me and tried to calm me. He told me about how much he cared for me, and said that with him I would never feel alone. He spoke soothingly and in his arms, I felt so relaxed. He picked me up, and carried me to the bedroom tucking me into bed. Before he pleaded with me to call him tomorrow but I told him that I would not make any promises.

The next day I chose not to call him. He called later that night asking for an explanation.

"Delois, what is going on? I thought you were feeling better about this."

"I know…I will call you tomorrow okay? I promise."
I did call him and that day we spent together. Like the night before, he tucked me into bed before he left. Leon in my apartment was beginning to be a regular routine. When he was assured that I was comfortable with having his company, he said that perhaps we could try making love again. We planned it this time so that I could be in the right frame of mind. It was about a week to the day of our decision and I bathed, oiled, and perfumed myself. I had on my

nightclothes when he arrived and he kissed me at the door. I brought out the wine he left for us previously, and I took out two wine glasses and placed them on the table. Three candles were lit and soft music was playing.

"What is all this?" Leon asked.

"Just getting in the mood" I responded.

He chuckled.

"I made dinner, would you like to have some juice?" I asked.

"No, I am not hungry." He said.

It was pretty late, too late for him to have dinner. I asked him if he would spend the night after making love. Leon told me that he would make that decision later. He picked me up and carried me to the bedroom. He laid me upon the bed gently and started taking off my clothes. His tongue slid across the surface of my torso, up to my breast. Then, he kissed me a few times before he began to speak. He asked if I had heard from my family and I told him that I had talked to my father. He wanted to know if I had talked to any of my girlfriends. I knew then that he wanted to know if I had told them about our relationship.

After much inquisition, I finally changed the subject. I wanted to know more about his practice. Of course, he didn't go into details, and then he slowly began to disrobe. He took off his shirt and placed it on a chair. Then, he took off his pants and folded them neatly across the chair to retain the crease. He took his keys and pocket-change from his pockets and placed them on the dresser. With nothing but his white briefs on he sat next to me on the bed. Then he stretched out on the bed. My heart was beating so rapidly I was sure he could see it through my nightgown. He began to rub my legs. He rubbed my thighs. Then, he rubbed the soles of my feet, my ankles, and the calves of my legs. He tickled my feet and kissed my ears and my neck. I did not touch him at all despite of the fact that he was practically naked. I couldn't bring myself to do it. He tried taking off my nightgown and I resisted. He kept pulling it up and I kept pulling it down. I could no longer repress my giggles and Leon realized I was playing with him. Finally, the mood changed.

I allowed him to pull up my gown; I laid there with my bare breasts facing him. I was wearing panties. He pulled me closer to him and raised me up. He began playing with my breasts and rubbing my back. He repeatedly told me how sweet my body was. I had petite breasts, very dainty and cute. He told me I had a cute stomach but I told him it could not be too cute because I had a large navel. When I was younger, a quarter had to be placed on it to reduce its size. He told me it was a cute little button and he liked it.

"You're skin is so soft and smooth." He said.

We were cuddling and he rolled me on top of him. We caressed each other and then I laid my head on his chest. He asked me how I felt and I told him that I felt okay. He pulled my panties down. But, when he tried to pull them off, I held on to them for dear life.

"Are you playing around again?" Leon asked.

"Yeah…I guess so." I replied.

I felt embarrassed, more like ashamed. I didn't know why either, but Leon assured me that there was no reason to feel that way with him. It wasn't the first time we had seen each others bodies. I told Leon that it had been a long time since we had seen each other's bodies. He started playing with my legs again and I bent one of my legs backward, trapping his fingers. The other leg I held straight up in the air. He asked why I was holding my leg so high and I told him that I was slightly ticklish; holding my leg up in the air was my way of coping. He tickled my feet and I laughed. I relaxed on his body, and he bean pulling my panties down, raising me up so that he could pull them down all the way around my ankles. He took them completely off and laid them on top of his pants. It was silent and he was so tender with me. Only the sound of our breathing could be heard. I felt the warmth of his body and this further relaxed me. Leon wanted to know how it felt lying next to his body. I didn't answer him, I just kissed his lips.

We caressed more passionately and he turned me over so that I was under him. He looked deeply into my eyes, and asked me to touch his body. I obliged, massaging his neck and shoulders. He told me that I could kiss him anywhere I liked and so I began kissing his chest. His hands slid under my shoulders and we embraced more closely. His body was so warm.

I looked around behind me as I saw Leon reaching for something. He was reaching for the condom. He told me that he wanted me to see how the condom was placed on his penis. He also had some kind of jell that he explained would be placed around my vagina and into the labia itself. He started caressing my thighs and began to massage my vagina while applying some of the lubrication. He explained everything he was doing. He said he would be as gentle as he could be and that he wanted the experience to be as painless as possible. He told me to relax and I told him that I couldn't. I was nervous when he spread my legs wide and began to insert his penis. I told him that I was feeling pain. He was insistent on working his penis into me. I felt pain, sharp piercing pain and I told him. He told me to relax and just try to enjoy it but I said that it was impossible to do so with so much pain. I told Leon that the experience was not feeling special and that I felt as if my body was being intruded upon. Then, he informed me that he had broken my "cherry."

"Cherry?" I asked, quite confused.

"Yes that's what the hymen is called, the flesh that blocks the entrance of the vagina." He responded.

Leon was very happy that he had broken my cherry. He said that this was a very special experience and he hoped that it was the same for me. He laid next to me and talked to me. He told me just how special this occasion was and that I would always be special in his life. I told him that I didn't feel special, I felt hurt, and I felt pain.

"Delois you are a novelty—"

"Novelty! I cut him off abruptly, "novelty?"

I felt the anger rise in me and pulled away from him on the bed.

"A novelty gets placed on the shelf and is replaced by a new *novelty*."

I grabbed my nightgown and sat up straight. I felt physical and emotional pain. Here is the man who took my virginity talking to me as if he had done me some great service. I did not want that, I realized then that I wanted love, undying love; I thought Leon would proclaim for me. I wanted him to talk about marrying me someday, loving me, wanting me by his side. I told him that I thought he would come to live with me in my apartment someday. He told me that I should concentrate on the experience at hand and not try to move to quickly. He took my hand in his and gently rubbed it across his face while he looked into my eyes. I could tell that he was sorry for his poor choice of words used to describe what he had just done. I relaxed a little and he laid down pulling me close to him so that I could nestle in the bend of his arm. We laid there for a while and then he took the covers and pulled them over us while we laid there facing each other. Soon after, I drifted off to sleep.

When I awoke, it was still dark outside; the sun had not yet come up. I found Leon next to me. I thought about what had occurred the night before and I began to weep in silence. Heavy tears ran down my cheeks and were absorbed into my pillow. "Here lays the man who took my virginity," I said to myself. I was scared, I did not know what to expect when he woke up. I was worried about it and began to cry some more. My sobs shook my body and Leon reached out half sleepily to touch my face. He retracted a wet hand and slowly opened his eyes to see my face. I cried harder and he pulled me close to him. He reassured me, telling me that everything was okay and not to feel bad about our experience. I didn't make it easy for him to console me I admit, but he finally coaxed me into expressing my true feelings.

I was not able to articulate the emotions that were raging inside me. Soon the sunlight was coming through the window. Leon checked the time and told me that he couldn't stay long. I laid there in silence looking up at the ceiling while he made his way across the room. I looked away from him and observed his actions out of the corner of my eye. He went into the bathroom and I heard him turn on the water for the shower. I continued to lay there stock-still.

When he came out of the bathroom, he returned and began to dry himself in front of me. He kept his eyes on me as he did these things and I stared at him for the first time. First, he put on his shorts, and then he put his undershirt on. He put on his pants and his dress shirt, tucking his shirt into his pants as he pulled them up. After he buckled his belt, he sat on the bed and put on his shoes and socks. Finally, he was all dressed and he stood in the middle of the room in front of me and asked me if there was anything I wished to say to him before he left. I remained silent and turned over on the bed. He came and tugged on my arm gently trying to get me to turn to face him. I refused and he asked if I wanted to talk, but when I said nothing he just told me that he loved me and made his way to the door. Before he left, he asked me to call him at work and left three different numbers where he could be reached. He also suggested that I stay at home and rest instead of going to work. Finally, he said goodbye, put on his jacket that was next to the door, and walked out. I heard him walk down the hall to the living room and out the front door.

I got up and ran a tub of hot water. It was about 7:30 A.M. I had nowhere in particular to go so I relaxed in the warm bath water thinking about what had happened. I was no longer a virgin. How was I going to deal with myself and the world? What was I going to do from this point forward? My virginity was very dear to me and now it was gone. I was a woman now, no longer a little girl but I was ambivalent about my own sexual maturation and about Leon. I was proud and ashamed; I hated Leon one minute and the next I loved him wanting to marry him and have his children. Later that day, Leon returned and when I opened the door, he stared back with an unreadable expression. Maybe it was surprise but whatever it was, he began to speak.

"You know," he said, "relationships must grow and one does not just find anyone to marry and have children with. Why do you feel that you need to have my children?"

"Well, why not?" I responded. "I mean, I though I was someone special in your life, I would think that this would be something you wanted."

"Right now," he began, "I'm concerned about your adjustment to womanhood. I have been concentrating all of my energy on that."

"Why are you telling me this? Why can't I have all of these other things with you?" I said.

"Listen, why don't I stay the night and we can talk about it."

It was the first time that Leon offered to spend the night with me. He told me not to worry he was not going anywhere. He grabbed me and held me on the side of the bed on his lap. I threw my arms around his neck and placed my body against his chest. In this position, we talked about the adjustments that would take place in our lives. We both needed a better understanding of all the things that had come to pass in our relationship and how we had gradually moved from being strangers, to friends, to lovers. He said that he was very proud of my being able to make the transition to womanhood. I was still uncertain about his intentions and whether or not this man who took my virginity deeply cared about me.

We cuddled the whole night but when I woke up in the morning, Leon had already gone to work. I got up and went to the bathroom. I took a long bath and tried to relax my mind that was running wild with questions, hopes, and fears. I returned to the bed, I didn't bother to dry off. I lay there, dripping wet, cold, and sobbing, hugging myself for both warmth and the feeling of loneliness that overcame me. Then I became angry. I was angry with Leon for being at work, not spending the day with me—a day that was very important because I wanted to relieve the stresses of my mind with him. I called his office but there was no answer. I had

something that I wanted to say to him something that only my heart

could understand. I called the second number and the third and still

received no response. Anger transformed into rage. I was furious

and I couldn't express what I was feeling to him at the time so I

wrote it down.

I decided not to go to work. I began to feel pain in the lower

part of my stomach, which spread to the rest of my body. I called in

sick and crawled back into bed where I cried myself to sleep. It was

around 2:00 P.M. when I woke up. I went to the bathroom and

looked at myself in the mirror. My eyes were red and swollen. I was

still angry at Leon and I called him, but this time he answered the

phone.

"Hello, Dr. Magin speaking."

"I am angry with you and what you did to me!" I screamed

hysterically beginning to cry again. "How could you take advantage

of me like that? Leaving me there by myself...I hope you feel

proud!"

He was silent, patient as I ranted and raved. When I was finished, he

began.

"I didn't just leave you there Delois I had to go to work. That's why I gave you three numbers to reach me so that you wouldn't feel the way you do now."

"Well I don't believe that for a second!" I said, and slammed the phone down.

He immediately called back and I slammed the phone down again. When he called back again, I hesitated and waited to hear what it was that he had to say. He told me that he would be over after work. He told me to call if I needed to speak to him again but I didn't call him for the rest of the afternoon.

He came by to see me as promised and spent the night. He kept telling me that he was not going anywhere and said that he would spend more time with me. He also asked me to stay home the next day, so I did. I wasn't eating, and I couldn't because I didn't feel well, my stomach started cramping. My menstrual cycle began not too long after the cramps, flowing like never before. This was reason enough for me to miss another day of work. Leon told me not to worry about money. He would pay my rent if needed and buy food. He told me to take as much time as I needed to recover. I took his advice and for about a month, I worried about myself and nothing else.

After my period ended, I still had stomach pains and decided to visit a hospital. I went to the emergency room of Kings County hospital. I was seen by a gynecologist and I explained to him that I was having stomach pains. I was told to lie down on the examination table and he felt around my stomach. He commented that it was very soft.

"Did you miss your period?" He asked.

"No I haven't" I replied.

"Do you have any children?"

"No I do not."

He felt around my stomach again and was not sure what the cause of my pain could be. He told me to take off my underwear, spread my legs open and place my feet in these things that looked like stirrups. I felt so exposed lying on a cold, stainless steel table spread eagle.

"Do I have to have my legs spread so far apart like this?"

"Yes it's the only way that I can see what the problem could possibly be."

There was no doubt in my mind that he could see the problem and any others that I was suffering from with my legs so far apart. I felt very uncomfortable on the table in the position that I was in. He kept adjusting my body downward on the table towards where he was facing me seated on a stool.

I craned my neck to see what he was doing with his hands and what he was preparing for me. He poked around inside my vagina with his fingers and I tensed up. I told him that what he was doing was painful but he continued. Then, he stopped poking and when I thought it was all over, he grabbed some chrome looking instrument. I asked him what he was going to do and he informed me that he was going to take a culture from me. He said that he would have to insert the instrument with his hand. Just before he did this, I kicked him and screamed.

"Wait! What are you doing?" He said with alarm.

"Wait nothing! That thing is going to hurt me!" I replied. "I don't want you to put anything else inside of me okay?" I said beginning to cry.

"I'm only examining you, it is standard proceed—"

"I don't want that metal thing inside of me!" I screamed.
"Who do you think you are?"

The nurse came into the room to see what the problem was.
She saw that I was crying and asked the doctor to step out for a
moment so that she could speak to me in private. When we were
alone, I explained to her that I had been in a convent and that I had
had sex for the first time a month ago. The nurse conveyed this
information to the doctor who felt sorry for me and apologized for
failing to explain to me everything that he was going to do.

"You should have told me that this was your first time here,"
He said smiling.

"Yeah, I know...I apologize for kicking you earlier" I
responded.

"No problem, but, it was quite a kick!"

I laughed and he continued, asking me where I lived and
whether or not I lived near a hospital. I gave him my address and he
filled out a prescription for my stomach pains. I asked him if he
would call me at some point and he affirmed. I apologized again, for
what happened and explained to him that I was still adjusting to my
recent sexual experience. I went on to ask if he had found any big

problems during his investigation. He told me that he did not and I gave him my phone number. He gave me his and promised to call soon in order to check on me.

A week or so later, while I was home alone, I decided to call the doctor. He said that he remembered me as a patient of his and asked if I minded him coming over to see me. I told him that I didn't mind and he said he would be over after work. When he arrived, he noticed that it was the same building one of his colleagues lived in. I told him that I did not have enough money to pay my doctors bills because at that time I was not working. He said that I was not a problem; he was examining me to see how I was. He said it was a house call and we both laughed at his play on words. After my checkup, we sat and talked. I told him about some of my experiences outside of the convent. He then told me that he would take me on as a volunteer patient free of charge and to call him if I needed anything, advice or otherwise. I thanked him and before he left, he gave me the number of one of his colleagues who lived in the building, just in case I needed to see a doctor for any reason.

Leon came over after work. I did not tell him that I had seen another doctor earlier that day and that I was given a prescription for pain medication. I didn't tell him how I was feeling but he noticed the change. I finally told him that I had been to see a doctor, took the pills out of the drawer and showed him the pills I had received. He told me that I would be okay and gave me a smile. He left soon after and promised to call me in the morning.

As time went on, he called more and I called less. I wanted to spend more time with him rather than speak on the phone, but he told me that he was not able to. In fact, over the next month he spent little or no time with me and spent more time at home. After much questioning, it was finally revealed to me that he was married. I couldn't believe it! It was a shock to know that I was the other woman, when all this time I was under the impression that I was his one and only. Leon broke my heart even further when he said that his wife was pregnant.

"Well, I began, if she can have a child for you why can't I?"

"No! he said, I just couldn't...I couldn't do that Delois"
I was frustrated; surely, he would grant me this one wish after devastating me so. I thought that I was going to explode with rage.

"Why didn't you tell me? Why didn't you tell me about her?"
I asked.

"I thought that I could keep my lives separate, that's all." He replied.

"You're a pig, a low down dirty, disgusting pig!" I screamed at the top of my lungs, and then, I called him every nasty name I could think of and that I never wanted to see him again before demanding that he leave. I was emotionally distraught. I loved him so much but I hated him just as much now. I left nasty letters with the doorman downstairs to give to Leon anytime he came to the building and whenever he tried, I wouldn't let him come upstairs.

I told the other doctor, Michael what happened to me. He comforted me as an older brother would and as our relationship grew closer, he began to call more often. This kept my mind occupied and off Leon, whose phone calls I repeatedly ignored. Michael would visit me in the day, he told me not to worry about money, that he would pay my rent. This was good seeing as how I had just broken up with Leon and still hadn't been to work. I was grateful for his assistance during this difficult time. Leon was still trying to get me back into his life. He sent me a money order for $200 to cover my living expenses, but I ripped it up. I called and said that I didn't want to see, or hear from him again. He began telling me how he was concerned about me; he wanted to continue our relationship as if nothing had happened. I told him that it would be better if he spent time thinking about his family instead of me. Eventually he stopped calling, but it wasn't before he sent another money order for $100 with an "I love you" note attached.

As I began meeting other men, I was no longer in a hurry to experience sex. Sex had not been one of the greatest experiences in my life, so it did not take much for me to push it to the back of my mind. I went as far as kissing and caressing but I wouldn't let any man go further than that. I would tell them that I was once a nun and I was still adjusting to life outside the convent. I found that when I told them this it was easier for me. Most of the men still wanted to be close to me and I was happy that I wasn't pressured into something that I didn't want to do.

As I adjusted more within relationships, I was more comfortable with becoming more intimate. If I had sex, it was on my own terms and I was happy to feel in control. There seemed to be many men who, after getting to know me, would begin to see me as some one potentially important in their lives. White, black, brown, they all hinted at marriage. I would call Michael and tell him of these proposals. I also told him of some who didn't even want to go to bed with me and wanted to marry me first. But, I wasn't interested in marriage and I was told by many jokingly that I was special, yet difficult.

I remember one gentleman by the name of Bert. Bert was rich, and a German Jew. He also wanted to marry me. Our dates included rides in his limousine around town, and trips to Broadway plays, ballets, concerts, and dinners at expensive restaurants. There were others, some of my boyfriends were from Brooklyn, Bedford-Stuyvesant and Flatbush. They were for the most part professionals who had accumulated some wealth. Some men wanted me as a trophy, which didn't sit well with me, seeing as how I wanted my own home and privacy. Men wanted me to move in with them but I began to assert myself, I told them that I was ambitious and that I didn't want to be controlled by them. It was this that influenced my decision to move from Brooklyn. I decided to move to Manhattan and share an apartment with my friend Louise, a top model in Manhattan, as I decided what I wanted to pursue. Louise had been responsible for my getting a scholarship to Barbizon.

Chapter Eighteen: The Return to Harlem

One Sunday in the midst of my predicament, a man called to see me. He said he was a friend of Dr. Harrington. Dr. Harrington was a friend and a member of the board of trustees of the New Future Foundation. A couple of days before the visit I hinted to Dr. Harrington my problems and he in turn mentioned it to his friend. Dr. Harrington had mentioned to me that he would talk to his friend about the possibility of taking one of the apartments.

I told him that I had no money but he insisted that his friend would do everything in his power to make sure I got the apartment. Dr. Harrington said that he understood what I was going through and appreciated the social work I had been doing. He asked how much I had been paying and that he would be more than happy to help me purchase an apartment at his mother's Co-op. I explained to him that I had no money to pay him back but he said it wouldn't be a problem. He said that he wanted more women to own property in the building. He also told me that owning the apartment would give me some stability. The only thing that I would have to be concerned with is maintenance. Even with that, it would still be cheaper than living on Fifth Avenue.

Dr. Harrington told me that if I could manage a certain amount, he would take care of the rest. He was very kind and gracious and told me that he was only giving back the assistance I had given to others throughout my life. I thanked him for coming at the time that I was really in need and in order not to offend him, I accepted his offer; even though I knew I probably wouldn't be able to come up with a portion of the money for the apartment. It was a beautiful apartment on Ten Park Avenue. He told me to go and inspect it, which I did. It had two large bedrooms which meant that one was to be shared by the boys while I was in the other bedroom with Ini, a beautiful screened in balcony, a spacious living room, a little kitchen and breakfast room, and two bathrooms.

"God is good," I said to myself filled with joy. "Here is the perfect place and it was brought to me on a silver platter." I called Sandra to tell her about my good fortune and then I got hold of the agreement and called John, a friend of mine who was a lawyer. John examined the agreement and told me that he thought it would be worth the investment since I was introduced by Dr. Harrington. Personally, I felt that I could not go wrong with the new place because of the involvement of Dr. Harrington; he was someone I could trust.

The following week something happened that overshadowed my decision to take over the place at Park Avenue. I found myself torn between going to Harlem and taking the apartment on Park Avenue. I reviewed the whole situation of my life and was beginning to feel that the circumstances of my life could be a good opportunity for me to return to Harlem and continue with my social work, which was what I knew how to do best. To be involved with my community was important, and I needed to get back to that. During my scouting, I found that there were many abandoned Brownstone houses in Harlem. This discovery brought in new ideas. I began to think that my predicament could be an opportunity for me to build an institute for children in Harlem where I wanted to live, among the poor, among my own. I thought I could live in a brownstone in Harlem rather than live on Park Avenue. I called Sandra who lived on Park Avenue and told her what was going on. I changed my mind about the place I got on Park Avenue, I was thinking of bigger things now. I told Sandra that I wanted to build a school for the children of Harlem and living on Park Avenue wouldn't allow me to do that. Sandra agreed that it would be best for me to go back to Harlem to live in order to make my dream a reality.

I thought that Harlem was the best place for me; eventually I made the decision that it was the place where I wanted to spend the rest of my life. After making such a tumultuous decision, I called Dr. Harrington and told him. He wanted to know why and I told him that it was based on my commitment to my people and Harlem was where I wanted to live and work. He reminded me that life would be more difficult for my daughter, and myself but, I told him that I would figure it all out somehow and not to worry about me, I would be fine.

My search for a place for my family to live ended at 477 West 142nd Street between Amsterdam and Convent. At last, I told myself,

I could live here. I didn't have to bother myself with when the next rent was due and so on. There was nothing attractive about the building except that it was of nondescript 19th Century European style architecture. Otherwise, it was an abandoned building by all definitions; the abode of junkies who slept in the hallway, with the pests, and swarms of flies who swarmed on their fecal matter. The stench of urine was nearly unbearable, and the strange characters that lived there would be enough to strike fear into any woman, many of whom would return home rather than cope with the conditions of the building. There was no running water, huge rats, and the area on Amsterdam was heavily trafficked with drugs. Convent Avenue was completely different.

There were black professionals who were homeowners, and beautiful brownstones. There were nuns who in a rectory across the street from a church. In the building that I was in, I chose to live on the third floor. Each apartment in the building had seven and a half rooms and two fireplaces. On each floor, an apartment was either facing the front of 142nd Street or the back. The apartment I chose faced the north side. It had many windows and I decided to move up high because of the condition of my daughter in order to make sure she received plenty of sunshine.

After I spoke to Dr. Harrington, I started preparing to move out of my apartment. I called Lula and told her that I needed someone to help me move and asked her if she knew anyone that could. She gave me the name of a Mr. Gainor who had a business in Harlem. He came in and brought his moving men. Lee and some of the students I knew from City College also came to help. Tony, another brother from Harlem, came to stay with the boys when I had to go to Washington D.C. because of my involvement with the International Year of the Child.

When I finally returned from Washington D.C., I moved to Harlem. Godfrey was upset because he did not want to live in Harlem. Having grown accustomed to the doorman service, maid service and the upper middle-class trappings of existence. The two boys rejected the idea of moving into an abandoned building; Tracey asked if I had lost my mind.

"Are things so bad that you can't ask grandma and grandpa for some money?" He asked me almost near tears.

"Sweetie you probably don't understand this now but there are things that some people just have to do on their own." I said. "I am an independent woman and I plan to remain so."

"Okay, but can't you ask someone to help you out? Why do we have to move to Harlem anyway ?" "We just do Tracey, we have to, I have to be apart of the Harlem community." Tracey hated the place. He complained about the rats, the unsanitary conditions, the roaches, and the lack of amenities. There were drunken men sleeping in the hallways and garbage strewn everywhere.

"At least there is plenty of space Tracey," I told him trying to convince him to look at the brighter side of things. "Now is the time to be strong you have to protect your auntie and be there for her."

That night Godfrey came home and helped Tracey and I move some of our things and clean one of the rooms in the apartment. He asked if he could visit some friends of his and I told him that it would be fine as long as he was back at 1 A.M. 1 A.M. rolled around and Godfrey didn't return. 2 A.M., 3 A.M., 4 A.M., and still no Godfrey! What was I going to do? He was placed in my care and he's a foreigner on top of that. At that point, I called the police department and tried to file a missing person's report. They asked how old he was and when I told them that he was 17, they said to give him more time.

Later that morning I called the FBI, Ambassador Salim and the U.S. embassy to tell them what happened. I had heard about the children of diplomats being kidnapped and held for ransom, I was hoping and praying that it wasn't the case with Godfrey. At ten o'clock the next day, Godfrey called. I began to scream at him on the telephone as the tears rolled down my cheeks.

"Godfrey how could you do something like that to me! I was worried sick!"

"I don't want to move to Harlem…I don't want to move into that abandoned house or any abandoned house with no hot water or electricity."

When we finished talking, I called everyone I had called previously to tell them that Godfrey was okay and that everything was alright. The next day, which was a Monday, I went to the Tanzanian Mission in company of Tony. I was told that Godfrey was there and when I arrived, I talked to him and the ambassador. "How could you do this to me Godfrey?" I asked on the verge of tears. Godfrey didn't answer. Tony started in on him. "How could you do this to your auntie after all she has done for you? You think you're a man? You are full of shit!" Godfrey remained silent and just stared at Tony.

"You're just a kid, a little kid running around New York City!"

Godfrey never uttered a word while Tony spoke. Then I began to cry, to sob.

"Why did you do it? You never gave me any trouble, why Godfrey? I would expect this type of behavior from Tracey but not you."

At that point, ambassador Salim spoke to Godfrey in Kiswahili, telling him that he must apologize, that it was no way to treat someone who was like a mother to him. The ambassador promised that Godfrey would be over later that day.

When Godfrey arrived, he immediately apologized for what he did. At the same time, he said that he wanted to leave. I pointed out to him that the U.N. general assembly would soon convene and that his father would be in town.

Paul, Godfrey's father, eventually came back to New York City. Naturally, I was upset, full of tears when I met him. He spoke to Godfrey and told me that he did not understand why Godfrey behaved the way he did. Paul also said that he was becoming a man, which was probably partly the reason for his change in behavior. He told me that Godfrey decided to move out. He would live at the YMCA and get a job in order to pay his rent. I understood, he was not a child anymore and it was time for him to start making his own decisions. Despite all that happened, Godfrey was still my child. When he would see me, he acknowledged me as a mother would expect. Paul let me know that I had reared him well and that he was proud of the man his son grew into.

"What do you expect a man to do? A man must leave his mother one day and he cannot be tied to her apron strings," said Paul.

I understood, but I still had to adjust to the differences based on culture. I had to let go of the thought of Godfrey as a child and introduce myself to the young man he became.

I was downtrodden and I had to work my way back up. My priority was Ini; I spent all the money I had in the bank on medical bills. Tracey suggested that I take Ini to the hospital but I said no, I wanted her to live in Harlem with us. Tracey said that the problem was too much for me to handle all by myself; he tried very hard to reason with me.

"That may be the case, but, I have come this far and I'm not going to give up now" I said to Tracey.

Tracey moved with me to Harlem. Here I was, with one son and a daughter. I realized that I was still hurt about Godfrey's decision. Tracey had a girlfriend now and wanted to spend a lot of time at her house. He wanted to run the streets and I was concerned about him getting involved in drugs and crime. It was a bad situation. There was no man in my life so I had some of the brothers from the community keep an eye on Tracey when I couldn't. I even passed out pictures and told them to scare him if need be so that he would want to go home but that wasn't necessary.

Tracey liked school and ended up spending most of his time there, especially in the library where he spent most of his time in the winter. He began to hang out with the Muslim brothers. I liked that because they provided him with discipline. He went to the mosque on Sundays and went to panel discussions about current events in the black community on his off time. At the liberation bookstore downtown, he became a frequent visitor. He wanted to learn more about Malcolm X and Martin Luther King Jr. He told me that one day he would be a president in Africa. He loved Dr. Kwame Nkrumah and was already talking about revolution. He criticized Godfrey saying that where he had gotten the chance to be a president or ambassador, he was shucking and jiving in America instead of trying to liberate African people.

Tracey was down with the revolutionary spirit that the young sometimes catch. I was glad that he had it instilled in him. I was glad to know what he was in to. I always knew where he was going or coming from. With Godfrey, it was always a guessing game but Tracey was vociferous. He talked about how the good die young and how he wanted to stay alive in order to see the change that he induced. His conclusion about some of the black leaders who died young was that they lacked intelligence. He asked me my opinion and I told him that I didn't know what to think, only that if he wanted to make it to old age, and do all the wonderful things that he desired, all he had to do was put his mind to it. Tracey told me that those were his intentions, and his mind was already set.

Tracey began to resent the fact that I spent too much time with Ini. The baby had not been well and I expected him to understand. One night, Tracey said to me "Auntie you don't have much time for me, you spend all your time with Ini." I said to him that it looked as if that I becoming a problem.

"I have to take care of my baby," I said. "You know that she really needs me. Maybe you are ready now to return to Florida. You can come back and visit on vacation."

"No, I don't want to go," said Tracey angrily.

"But it would be nice if you went, don't you want to see your mother? You are always talking about her and your father. Your father, your little sister and brother, don't you want to see them?"

"No, I don't. I want to stay here."

Not to long after this I noticed a change in Tracey's behavior; he started acting out. He refused to do what I told him to and disobeyed me frequently. I had to put my foot down.

"Tracey you have to go home now. I can't go out searching for you when you should be home. You are defying me all the time now. You are not going to school or the library. I don't know where you are half the time and I can't have this. I am calling your mother."

"No auntie, no! You don't have to do that. Plus, I can't leave now I have been going to school here."

"Then you call her and ask her what arrangements can be made."

He called his mother and I spoke to her first. She said that it was kind of me to keep Tracey all of these years. Then Tracey got on the phone, he began to cry. His worst fears were confirmed and he was told that he had to return home. He told his mother that he wasn't going, he was staying here. That's when I heard her loud and clear over the phone.

"You listen here Tracey! You have a mother that is alive and well, a whole family that is! You pack your bags right now and get on a plane tonight! Don't make me come up to New York City to take you back home."

"But mom I need time to say goodbye to my friends, can't I do that please?"

"Okay, if it's alright with your auntie then fine, but don't you dare stay longer than you have to you hear me?"

I told her that it was okay for him to do that and we agreed that by the end of the week, he would be on a plane.

Tracey, Ini, and I were waiting in the airport for Tracey's plane.

"Auntie, you know you are a good auntie and I love you very much." Tracey said as he hugged me and kissed me. "I hope I didn't give you a hard time and I pray that Ini will get well and I will be able to take her to the park like other children."

"You stay in touch with me when you get home, you hear me?"

"Of course auntie how could I lose contact with you? I mean, you taught me so many things…you taught me how to read!"

"I know, and there is no limit to what you can do if you put your mind to it okay?"

"I still want to be a president in Africa."

"I have no doubt that you will. Continue to do well in school okay."

"Yes auntie I will."

"I'm going to miss you Tracey, a lot."

"Auntie you gonna make me cry talking like that. I can't cry in the airport there may be some girls looking."
We both laughed when he said this but then I started to cry.

"Auntie, come on you are going to get me choked up. I'm not a sissy you know."

"I know Tracey sorry for getting all emotional."

"It's okay auntie it's me that I'm worried about."

Tracey kissed Ini and me and then, he said goodbye. He told me that we would both be in his prayers; he kept waving until he got to the plane.

When I got back home later that day, I called him and he had arrived in Fort Lauderdale. I told him that I missed him already.

"Well, auntie I don't miss you yet, I just got here." He said laughingly. "But soon I know, I will call you need you, you won't have to call. You will probably get sick of speaking to me!"

After speaking to Tracey, I talked to his mother for a little while. Then I just sat for a while. It was just Ini and me now.

Chapter Nineteen: Going to Africa

My motivation for going to Africa in the first place was to go home. This was to be a sojourn to what I knew was my ancestral home and what I felt was my spiritual home.

Identification with Africa for African-Americans may come about in many ways. For some, the identification comes about through consciousness awakened through the Civil Rights Movement. For others, it comes about through curiosity about Africa, reading, traveling, and discussing with others who were knowledgeable about Africa's glorious and rich cultural contributions. For me it came about from my earliest childhood experience. I recall telling my father that the children in school had called me ugly. I knew that children were often brutally honest in a self-centered way. My very dark skin, broad, bulbous nose, short kinky hair that did not grow long and very prominent cheekbones, had a very profound affect on my perception of self. Through the wisdom of my father, I overcame any potential problems accepting myself with some simple wisdom.

"Beauty is in the eye of the beholder," my father said. "Don't you ever forget that Delois."

At a very impressionable age, my father's words meant everything. I was able to explain away much of the potential self-hatred. It allowed me to put aside my looks as real issues and pursue a health ego.

"Beauty comes from within; it is the cultivation of what is inside that determines beauty."

What are fathers for if not to help ugly children build their self-esteem? I certainly did, and I was lucky. Less fortunate children would not have been able to cope psychologically. They wouldn't have been able to put a self-beautification process into practice, in order to exhibit their internal beauty. It was the quest for internal beauty that led me to the convent; it was the same quest that led me to Africa.

If taken separately, my looks are composed of color and contour adaptations performed by nature as life-enhancing responses to the climate of a warm environment. I look African. I am African in all ways, and sometimes, even more so than other Africans do. This I also learned at a young age. Armed with the wisdom of my father and possessing a healthy mind and ego, I was quick to pay attention to the pictures of Africans even when I was in kindergarten.

These people looked like me, millions of them! Sisters, mothers, aunts, and neighbors all with features like mine. I was sure they did not go around calling each other ugly. The fact that I looked African worked wonders for my social climbing in the United States. As I said, my work with multiethnic programs took me frequently to the United Nations. I dressed the part for each occasion, usually for the General Assembly meetings. I became very familiar with the guards, and floor directors there, who, without even asking, assumed I was part of an African mission or embassy. With this impunity, I was free to become involved with the affairs of the United Nations and particularly with the African representatives.

I knew that a strong and comprehensive understanding of the youth affairs of African nations was an important part of my multiethnic concept. It would give me a healthy perspective on the African-American youth affairs by sorting through the commonalities of the youth of the African Diaspora. I was sure that only wisdom and a greater understanding of African-American youth would result from such experience. The Nigerians at the United Nations and at schools in New York City became close friends of mine. They too were interested in the international affairs of the African Diaspora and were happy to see African-Americans represented in the quest for understanding. Later, diplomats of the United Republic of Tanzania's Mission to the United Nations became interested in what I was doing in New York City. Africans from all over the continent were my guests at 24 Fifth Avenue. It was because of my credibility as the founder and president of the New Future Foundation; my presence at the United Nations and my multiethnic work in the city resulted in the Tanzanian ambassador, Paul Rupia, entrusting his son, Godfrey, in my care. I was also given an invitation to travel and study in Tanzania. My Fulbright scholarship was also awarded for this purpose.

This was my first trip in many years to Africa. I had already traveled to Egypt and other regions in North Africa. Now, it was time for me to go east, west, and south. I wanted to observe and study their style and behavior in education. I wanted to incorporate what I observed in Africa into the educational program I was planning for Harlem, the Harlem everyone knew and traveled to, from Mother Teresa, to Queen Elizabeth. Harlem itself is like a village frequented by the likes of Malcolm X, Marcus Garvey, Martin Luther King Jr., or any other heroes. I was not going to Africa to trace my roots, there was no need, I knew where I belonged, where I originated. I simply wanted to go home, and not to the continent that was erroneously depicted in the movies; Tarzan and Jane were so absurd, the "king" and "queen" of the African jungle? This was fallacious, and I was glad that I saw past this at an early age.

When I arrived in Tanzania, I was able to meet with Mwalimu President, Julius Nyerere. He greeted me in causal attire then, he led me to his porch where we sipped lemonade. I talked to him about my big ideas, not only to save children, but also, to become an ambassador for goodwill. I spoke about my future leadership in Harlem and the difficulties that I must overcome as a woman in a male dominated arena. President Nyerere enjoyed our conversation and allowed my spirit to reign. He had fatherly warmth about him that reminded me of my own father. Our relationship grew close and I was able to meet with him again before I left. This meeting took place in his village and I told him then about my plans for Africa, Tanzania specifically.

"I challenge you to go south; I noticed that you haven't traveled to South Tanzania yet," said President Nyerere.

"Well, I will go, I am going south." I responded.

It was difficult to go south, but I was able to talk to the pilots that were with me during the trip. I let them know I needed a lift.

My work and explorations in Tanzania were made easy, not just by the government, but also by the people. The people paved the way for my visits to their villages; I was able to see their schools. I was given permission to use the Tanzanian VIP plane, and was dropped off and picked up, on my own schedule. I was able to move about easily, getting my research completed on the "self-reliance" educational system there. President Nyerere wanted me to see the country; he was not hiding anything from this future leader. He especially wanted me to interact with the children, "feel their pulses," as he put it. I was accepted as a member of the country and I felt as if it was home. I was a daughter of Africa; I flowed freely from place to place and as I was doing that something great happened. Villagers speculated about my nationality. I was Ugandan to some, West-African to others. I was thought to be from Nigeria and Ghana, Bukoba and Mwanza; the people were constantly trying to match my features with some particular country or tribe. I was able to go to Arysga and Monduli, still doing my research there among the Masai. I was causal walking around, in some cases filming, even though I had to get the permission of the Masai in order to film. I couldn't just take a camera into someone's village and record their every move. Getting permission was no problem and I had more material for my research.

The people spoke to me in the tribal language and became quite upset when I wasn't able to respond accordingly. My colleagues translated for me and explained to the villagers that I was from America. They explained that American was a far of land inhabited mostly by whites, which catalyzed commotion.

"She is not white; there is nothing white about her. Herpana zungu!" they cried.

"She if from America," my colleagues began. "Her ancestors left Africa as slaves and voyaged to America, where she now resides."

After a short time people crowded around me, examining me. They concluded that there was no way I could be anything else but African. Then the young warriors, the Moran, began to gather around me. They were going through their initiation period and wore black robes with white masks to cover their faces. This was part of the ritual of coming into adulthood, and it was made very clear that we would not film them. Not even the senior warriors bother them during that time as they were proving their manhood. They got closer to me and I did not know what to do. I was told that whatever the Moran decided to do, no one would hold them back. There were about seven to ten Moran among those gathered around. "Should I run?" I thought, "Should I bow, pray, scream out?" The Moran stared and they were not half-stares or self-conscious stares. They were stares that seemed to penetrate my very soul. They did not blink, and the few minutes that they took to stare seemed like an eternity.

I was alone in the circle. My colleagues had been separated from me somehow and I had to keep in mind that I was a woman. I thought about the stories one hears about the Masai. Men can take women for their wives if the so choose and I thought that perhaps this would happen to me and I would never get back to America. I thought, "Well, this is it." "How am I going to explain the fact that I became a Masai bride to my relatives and friends?" Perhaps I would be stolen by one of the Moran who wanted to prove himself. I thought that I would not be found ever again, I would be cut off from any contact with the outside world. I began to pray. However, at that point, I did not know for sure if I was praying for or against this possibility. They were extremely handsome fellows, virile and manly. As I became more at ease, I stared back. I looked at their facial features as this was my first real encounter close-up. I looked at their bone structures, their long extremities and their dark skin, which looked as if it were as smooth as silk. I decided that whatever happened I would not back down, even though I had no control over the situation, I was outnumbered and had no choice in leaving. I thought to myself that I might as well enjoy the situation, so I began to think of whom I would marry if I did have the choice.

"The audacity of this one to stare back at us, who does she think she is?" I imagined them saying as they exchanged glances with one another and then back at me. I had already decided to challenge them and exuded as much pride as I could muster. I started batting my eyelids hoping one of them would respond. I was looking for some kind of warmth and acknowledgement. I was searching for their understanding but it was never displayed. I thought that if I blinked my eyes long enough at least one of them would play along. They did not give me that invitation there was simply no response. They continued to stare though, looking me up and down and talking amongst themselves. At length, one of them became the spokesperson for the group and he spoke very forcefully, dashing his hand downward as he spoke. Of course, I did not know what his words or gestures meant. I wanted to know what was going on regarding me. I was told that the group thought of me as "pure Masai" and they concluded that I had been kidnapped and were quite happy that I had returned. Again, my translator and companions explained that I was from America and the Moran responded repeatedly with, "Hapana!" (She is not white). They claimed that they did not know how I had gotten lost, perhaps I had wondered away, but they were happy that I was back where I belonged.

The conclusions of the Moran led them to retrieving the village elders. The elders arrived and that same day they named me Naewoaang "One who has been away but who has returned to her people." They understood that I was still in the midst of my research and that I would have to leave the village for a time, but that I would

return before I left for America. They wanted to know when I would

be back, when I would be returning home, when I would be

returning to stay forever. They informed my colleagues that they

would be preparing a celebration upon my return to the village. My

colleagues went on to explain to them that I was similar to their

Sokoine, warriors who worked for the government. With this

development, they thought that I was on a mission with the Prime

Minister Sokoine.

I left them to continue my sojourn to other countries. I went

to Zambia where I met with President Kenneth Kaunda. We dined

together, and had a press conference for two and a half hours. As a

daughter of Africa and, as a future leader, talking with an elder like

Kenneth Kaunda was very rewarding. It was then that I realized I

had a responsibility to my own people. As I traveled, further south

to Zimbabwe and Malawi, which is a skip and a jump away from

Johannesburg, I was issued, for one year, a multi-entry visa to travel

South Africa. As I went from border to border, I was always

accepted. The only limitation to my travels was the fact that I could

not speak the languages. Everywhere I went in Africa after that, I made it clear to the locals that I was Masai. I was able to hold my head up with a lot of pride for having been claimed by a group of people who said that I was one of them.

When I returned to Tanzania and Dar es Salaam, I wanted everybody to come to the celebration, which was being prepared for in my honor. I sent President Nyerere an invitation, which went to his village, Butiama. As I traveled to Ruwanza and on to Bukoba, and Zanzibar, I paraded in the knowledge of the celebration that was in store for me. Soon I was going to be a full-fledged Masai! The time came for the most glorious day of my life. It was like the turning of a new leaf in the chapter of living. It was the beginning of something very deep. For five days, they had been preparing this celebration, and there were certain things I was asked to do. I was asked to spend more time in Arusha. I was also asked to spend more time throughout the Masai region and to visit all of it.

With my colleagues and the government officials, I began the journey from Arusha Town in a Land Rover. We had spare gas, tires, and an expert driver who knew the Masai region like the back of his hand. The experience was breathtaking. I saw Masai walking across the plains in the shadow of the sunset accentuating their tall outlines.

The glow of red clay in their hair and the waving of the garb, everywhere I turned there were beautifully sculpted bodies. The sights left me in ecstasy of the wonder of God's creations, the simplicity of the Masai; they were one with nature. Weary legs of Masai men rested against those of their brothers, seemingly attached as one uses the other as a leaning post. The companionship between the Masai was unprecedented, everyone was apart of the larger Masai family. This was everyday life for them.

For hours we drove. We saw the land of the Masai in all its glory. We stopped to rest from time to time looking beyond the plains, where we say a crater, a beautiful spot where a volcano once stood but has since then returned to the Earth. It is hollow and we get closer, we drive higher above sea level. Going around the mountain was the most frightening experience of my life. There was nothing to see but dew and dense fog. Here the mood of the land transformed. The curves were sharp and the drop downward from the Cliffside was steep to say the least. I leaned over the edge of the truck to see downward and every time I did, I screamed at how nothing but the skill of the driver and God's Holy will kept us on the right course. If someone tried to describe the land, he or she would have had to compare it with the Garden of Eden. It was beautiful, lush green with heavy vegetation. I was positive that this crater was where humankind originated. No number of horticulturalists could have produced such a sight. It was truly God made.

I was between rapture and fear, I prayed the whole time. I asked when we would get to where we were going, and the driver seemed quite happy. He assured me he had made the trip many times before; I did not have to worry. I was happy that he was an expert, but that did not dismiss the fact that we were on a mountain. We rested again when we arrived at one of the stations along the way, which had been placed there for tourists to be serviced. It was at this station that we came upon other travelers. They were anthropologists, historians, and others who rode in an open truck. It did not seem like it offered much comfort or safety like the Land Rover did. I was glad that I wasn't in that open truck. As we continued our journey down into the crater, we could observe other travelers who, having gone before us, were now covering the distance, which we would soon be covering. My heart was in my mouth. The winding down into the crater was no more comforting than the trip up its rim. I did not want to look over the side even though I wanted to see the beauty of this place; the sharp jutting cliffs keep me glued to my seat.

The guides thought that it would be a good experience for me if we stopped at the edge of the crater before entering it; there was a Masai village there. Who else but the Masai would be brave enough to live not only in the wilderness among the wild animals, but also on the edge of a crater? There was commotion in the village about a certain cheetah. This cheetah was killing Masai sheep. There was a little anxiety about removing the cheetah, but they wanted to prevent further killing of their precious flock. They did not intend to hurt the animal; instead, they wanted to take it far away, so that their sheep would be out of harms way. I was astounded by the idea of a killer animal nearby and the course of action that was being considered by the villagers. I would have been very worried about the children or the elders of the community with this dangerous animal lurking about. The guides asked me if I wanted to see how they would transport the animal away from the village. This was going to be quite an experience for someone who had never been close to a cheetah before. I began to get excited about the prospect of seeing the Masai accomplish this feat. I thought to myself, "As long as the cheetah is not near me, it will be quite an experience to see how this animal is transported."

The Masai has a truck and a cage; we followed them. We traveled down like we were traveling from heaven to hell in the same trip, except, I could not imagine hell being as beautiful. We traveled miles, racing behind the truck that carried the cheetah. They wanted me to see the release of the cheetah, I had my camera ready, and I was terrified! At that very moment, they released the latch, and I captured this magnificent animal on video. The Masai did not get out of the truck, but had a cord extending from inside of the truck to the latch. It was interesting to note that the release was done by remote control. When the cheetah jumped down to the ground, he quickly looked around before taking off like a bolt of lightening. "Run cheetah! Run, Run!" I screamed excitedly as it galloped away at top speed. Soon it disappeared across the plains.

We were well within the crater now; I had never been this close to wild animals in my life. This was an animal's domain; we were now in their world, a place not yet disturbed by humans and their destructiveness. I had never seen such large snakes as they slithered around the trees. We got very close to the lions in the Land

Rover and drove by a lake where the rhinos were resting. There were more varieties of birds than I could count, and elephants were grazing under the blazing sun. All existed naturally, in perfect harmony with each other. It is the kind of setting that is difficult to describe; the only way to something as wonderfully breathtaking as the experience I had would be to see it with ones own eyes.

Returning from the crater was a meditative experience. I must enter here an account of the late Prime Minister Sokoine whose sudden death was at about the same time I was awaiting the celebration for me given by the Masai. Sokoine was a warrior well loved by his people. I have never seen a nation mourn the death of anyone like they did for Sokoine. I recalled the deaths of John F. Kennedy and Martin Luther King Jr. and neither death were mourned as this one was. The way the country was moved by his death was an experience within itself. I requested as part of the preparation for my own celebration, to visit the home of Sokoine. I went to the home where he was buried, and visited the home of his mother and his wives. The family had declined a state burial at a national shrine; both the immediately family and the tribe, to which he belonged, requested that his remains be sent home.

As I moved through the Masai land, I did it with the oneness of the Masai who embraced me. Engareonlmotony, Armeru, the mountain called me as the child, the infant of my people. The mountain froze me; it had me as the wind captures the dust as I moved through Monduli land. I had to return to the village, the village that awaited me and took me in as one of its own. As the Land Rover rushed over the plains of Monduli, it rushed me to where I belonged. Engareonlmotony was in the distance, I could hear them chanting, "Naewoaang, Naewoaang, Naewoaang return to us." Seeing the tall outlines of men, women, and children made my heart thump. I was waiting to greet, and embrace, especially the elders. I could not wait to see my people their chants were like animal sounds coming from the human voice, sounds I will never forget. Paulo Siriwa greeted me and showed me the path where I would walk to meet the villagers. On both sides of the path, there were branches of trees prepared showing that this was a special occasion. I was escorted to the village and I moved to a new rhythm of life, I felt my new self. I was anxious and excited; it is hard to explain everything I felt in that one moment. The air was filled with chanting and praying, animal like screams all for me, and a long life among my people.

The feeling I had cannot be translated, it was a spirit and all I could do was enjoy it, savor this oneness with my people. I moved toward the open court where they gathered, humbled like a small child in this royal festivity. I began to cry, an emotional outpouring of all my senses taking in this beautiful occasion. Some of the villagers cried as well saying, what was later translated for me as, "She is truly one of us." A bond of love was sealed between them and me. I was at a loss for words, and I could only be still; I accepted and acknowledged the village as my land, my heritage, my family. As the ceremony continued, they placed me in front of the yard. There was a long table with ointments and decorations. The chief of the village, and the council of elders greeted me and I took my place among them. The program began. The women sand in front of me and they thanked the spirit God for bringing me safely back to them. They prayed to the spirit God for Nyerere that he would have the foresight to accept my return to my people. They prayed that he have a long life, and that I would walk as a true daughter of Tanzania and Masai. The children sang in front of me, their voices ringing in harmony like the calls of birds.

I had to take the responsibility of leadership among my people and the council took me before one of the village elders. I knelt before Mzee an elder who was 110 years old. He blessed me and made sure that as the women closed in on me there was an elder present to witness my new birth and life among my people.

"If the warriors would not dance for you, I would, so all would know you are a daughter of our people and as such, you must become a leader among your people, our people," said the elder.

He told me to promise him that wherever I went, I would always return home.

"You will be blessed with many cows if you teach the children," he said. "You must learn the ways of our people give this knowledge to the young but, you have to be patient; everything will not be learned in a day."

They placed a black gown on me that touched the floor and tied it to my waist. This gown symbolizes the Masai tribe. There was also a purple cape placed around my shoulder and tied in a knot. The donning of the Masai beads by the women of the village was their tribute to our new sisterhood. With great meaning, they placed their handiwork around my neck. My hair had already been braided and beaded by one of my sisters of the village. My hair had been oiled with cow oil, as was the practice among my tribe. For the time being my ears were not pieced. The piercing would be performed by village women and healed under their care upon my return.

I was taught how to eat with my people. As I sat among the senior elders and my sisters at the feast of festivity, they passed me the meat of the goat, which was roasted for this occasion. We all ate from a large bowl. We shared the oneness of the family, united in our dining. I dipped my hand into the bowl and helped myself to small chunks of meat. I was told that the ribs, the sweetest part of the animal, had been especially roasted for this occasion. I learned that the best part of the meat was where the lean and fat mixed. I learned how to chew properly for the first time, but it took me a while to get accustomed.

I was still on my first piece of meat while everyone else had moved onto other pieces. My people, realizing I was young among them cut my meat into smaller chunks, the same as one would do for an infant. They were aware of my being new to their culture and were very patient with me; after all, I could not learn about all this in a day!

We drank milk and I was offered other things to drink that they thought I would be accustomed to. As they passed around the drink, I simply said "no thank you." Again, my people were patient with me explaining to me that in their culture there wasn't a "no thank you." If you were offered something, that you didn't want or need, you simply passed it to the next person. I also learned that I should never eat alone. If I could not find someone to eat with me within my house, I must go outside and eat in case there is a hungry passerby in which case I would be able to share with him or her. I learned other things among my people but they are very dear to me and I promised that I would never share the most sacred traditions of the Masai.

As I stumbled trying to say my first words in their language, members of my family repeated the words correctly until I was able to say it exactly as they did. I became frustrated with some of the words but again, I was reminded to be patient and that I would learn in due time. We moved from one celebration to the next and the whole time, my thoughts were on the village elder. I kept reflecting on how badly I wanted to see him. I even asked some of the others if it would be possible to see him twice in one day. I wanted to see what the young warriors, the Moran were up to. They did not join us at the feast, and I later learned that this was because women were present. They ate amongst themselves and senior warriors only. I asked permission to see them and it was granted.

I went to see where they ate and as soon as I arrived, everyone stopped. I was not supposed to see them eating but it was told by one of the elders who accompanied me that I just wanted to be in their presence for a moment. I soon returned to the elders, the council, and the women. By this time, the children had returned to school to have their lunch, but they were going to return for the next part of the celebration. As I enjoyed the festivities, I noticed the two government pilots in charge of my transportation standing off to the side. Being from a different tribe, they never witnessed a Masai celebration. They were in awe, overwhelmed by everything that was happening, and filmed the great festivities in action.

It was time for the warriors to perform the great dance of celebration to show their strength, bravery, and passion for protecting their village. They were to dance one by one. They began to chant. The warriors did not use drums; they used their voices and stamped their feet in rhythm. They began to jump and chant, sing and dance for me. As they jumped to show their warrior spirit, they whipped their heads in a circular motion swishing their hair. I was astounded. "These brave warriors, protectors of their village, doing all this for me," I thought. As the warriors danced, the women joined. I soon learned the movements. It was all joy and laughter, a great simplicity among my people.

As the day ended, the whisper of the young captains came; "we must now return to Dar es Salaam." I had a final request, to speak again with the Mzee who blessed me. With special permission from the council, I was able to return to his boma. I never entered because once you enter, you cannot leave out right away; it is not acceptable.

The Mzee came out of his boma and I promised him would return and spend time with him in the boma. We talked in the yard among the cows. I will never forget the alertness he had for his 110 years, a clarity of vision. He spoke to me in the tribal language and one of the villagers was appointed to translate. He told the translator verbatim, not what the translator "thought" I ought to know. As the translator did his best to do so, I noticed that the sentences were much shorter. It was very difficult for me to remove myself from the Mzee in the yard as I listened to his wisdom. I had to remain with the elder until he gave me permission to leave but I did not mind because I was enraptured, captured by his enlightenment. The Mzee made it known to me that I was wealthy as a Masai. He said that I must return to my people and that when I did, he would have a gift waiting for me, a stool made by his own hands. At that moment, I did not want to leave. I began moving away slowly after he gave permission for me to, wordless, not wanting to say something like goodbye, which seemed like a permanent state of being now.

During the time I traveled with the pilots to the airstrip, I talked about what happened. All I could talk about was the time when I would return to my people. Before we left the village, the pilots agreed we would circle the village as I had told the villagers I would. It must have taken two hours for us to get to the airstrip, get the signal to takeoff and actually fly over the village. I kept telling the pilots to hurry.

"We must not keep them waiting!" I said. "They must see the plane before we head for Dar es Salaam. I must see the village from the sky."

We took off gaining altitude and began turning around toward the village. As we approached, I asked repeatedly, "will they see us? Will they see that it is us?" The pilots assured me that they would.

"We're there," said one of the pilots.

"Where?" I asked.

"Directly over the village, look down."

I looked below and at first and I didn't see anything. The captains flew low enough so that I could see the villagers waving. We circled the village three times and then, we headed for Dar es Salaam. It was a moment of sadness for me, a moment of leaving a part of myself with my people, a moment that could not be expressed in words. I became silent. The copilot turned to se what was wrong and I explained to him that I missed my family. The tears welled up in my eyes but the pilots reassured me that I would return some day. I was just going to be gone for a short period to accomplish my goals that the old man spoke of. The tasked placed upon me by the old man loomed in front of me. I began to ask myself questions.

Am I a blessed one endowed with the good fortune to have seen the world in a very special way? Will I enlighten them? Am I the one chosen to free my people from the bondage of injustice and from racist regimes? I thought of the many problems confronting my people on the continent of Africa and, at the same time, I thought of the goodness despite it all. What role did I play for mother Africa? What role is meant for me in the struggle for my people?

It seemed like a quick journey to Dar es Salaam as I heard the pilot announce that we were preparing to land. It was like waking from a dream. I began to put myself back into reality. This new reality now contained pride of being a Tanzanian and of being a Masai. At the airport, I thanked the pilots and they hugged me.

"Do you really know what has happened to you? It is something that I didn't witness before today, celebration in the Masai tribe. Now you can feel it, you are a Masai!"

As we drove from the airport to the hotel, I talked with the pilots about having another feast. When I walked into the hotel, all the people there knew that I was now a Masai through Radio

Tanzania. For days, I walked in my ceremonial clothing. I was seen all over the city in the garb of the Masai. When the Masai of Dar es Salaam received word, they came to the hotel to greet me and to rejoice with me. The Masai warriors who were in Dar es Salaam did not call me to see if I would see them, instead they came to see me.

The months preceding my leaving Tanzania were very difficult. It became hard to accept the idea that I had to leave. My research was over and it was indeed time for me to return home. It was time for me to return to that now foreign land I had left. As I prepared to leave, I said, to myself that I wouldn't leave Mother Africa. I remember what the Mzee told me.

"This is home wherever you may go." He said. "Your spirit will remain among our people even when your body leaves."
I called a Masai brother after packing to leave because I decided not to take all of my gifts from the village. I repacked and left with my Masai brother the most important gifts; the ones blessed as a symbol of a new life for me in Africa. This act represented a new direction my being had to step into. With this act, my mind was at rest. It was a symbolic act of declaring that I would never be separated from my people again. Before I left Tanzania I had the opportunity to return

to my village. I informed my people that after I finished my travels to other African countries, I would return to a very special village in New York City, a village called Harlem. There I would be embraced as their sister of Africa, their sister of Tanzania and their sister of Masai.

John F. Kennedy Airport gave me my first real taste of culture shock. A young woman newly invited into the Masai, I was bound to have my senses shaken upon arrival to the bustling airport. That was however, part of the travel experience, it had to be accepted, what a shock it was! The hard reality of my daughter Ini, the abandoned building transformed, and all of my school and professional responsibilities lay at my feet waiting for me to take them up again. Couldn't everyone see the change within me? Why did they to continue to treat me as if I went nowhere? I began to busy myself finding refuge and understanding for my recent experiences. Where could I identify with persons who might understand how I felt about Africa? I needed people around me who understood me as a person transformed. I saw that I could contribute not just to Africa, Tanzania, and the Masai, but also to people of the African Diaspora. I felt that Harlem, the island nation because of my extended family in Grenada, as well as my village in Africa, as being sites that would complete the institute I was planning.

I sought the company of Africans at the Tanzanian Mission to the U.N. I wanted to be in an African milieu. As the time for the United Nation's anniversary and the Nairobi Women's Conference approached I got very busy. I was in Nairobi during the pre-planning for the conference, I identified strongly with the work of the Africans, and African-Americans who were planning for the conference. This also put me in the African milieu I was seeking. I wanted to share my experiences in Kenya and my involvement with the women; I traveled all over the continent and in doing so, was able to observe the status and progress of the women there. I organized information updates for African-American women regarding the upcoming women's conference. I went on the radio, WLIB to discuss my experiences in Africa and the possible role African-American women could play at the conference. We helped Queen Mother Moore, who would represent those of us who would not be going to the conference, raise money for the trip to Nairobi. While there, I had met with the chairperson of the Women's Nairobi

Conference, Margaret Kenyatta. These experiences not only put me in a position to help other African-American women understand the importance of the conference, but it also allowed me to retain my spiritual connection with Africa. I made the decision that from this time on, I would be actively engaged in the affairs of Africa and the African Diaspora. It was in this way I was able to bridge the gap between the women of African and the Women of Harlem without propaganda and with understanding.

The preparations for the fortieth anniversary of the United Nations, was also an opportunity for me to build a bridge between Africa and African-Americans. I knew that Mwalimu Nyerere was going to be in New York City for this event. He was to be present at the U.N. to give his last address as President of Tanzania before his planned retirement. This was to be an opportunity to thank him publicly for the contribution. We invited one elder of Harlem to be present with us when we presented President Nyerere with a commemorative plaque, which also expressed our appreciation of him as a leader. My own joy and spirit of Africa was renewed while waiting at the U.N. with the African Ambassadors to enter the General Assembly to hear Mwalimu Nyerere's last speech. We sat among the Tanzanians and experienced the kinship I had among the Masai. I was there with the elder Queen Mother Moore and another sister from New York City.

When president Nyerere spoke, I was in awe, the awe of his words and of seeing him again. He spoke with such vigor and directness. I was moved by his simplicity and humility, his strength and character. He was a giant in my time, determined to make a difference. He stood up for what he believed in showing courage in his thin, weak looking frame. He was not afraid to make a mistake.

"We may be small, we may not have all that we need, but we will take a stand for what we believe!" said President Nyerere. He may have been stepping down but he certainly wasn't giving up. He liked the idea of young people like me actively involved in making the world a better place. It was with honor that an elder of Harlem and I, as well as the sister who accompanied us, presented President Nyerere with a plaque expressing our gratitude for his leadership. He kissed me on the cheek as a father would a daughter, as happy to see me, as I was to see him. Such a sweet reminder of my people back home in the motherland.

PROLOGUE

As an elder I long to tell my story. I share with you , The Hip Hop Generation, The X Generation, the superhighway generation that move at the speed of light and miss every other beat, the Generation they call the poor and the powerless that are mis-educated in the wilderness of life. I echo to all of you to digest these pages, reflect on it and learn from my experiences,.. As you live your life I hope that you would be able to feel me that once was like you in any given situation as you reach your heights. I want you to be with me as I reveal more to come. May God take a liking to you!

- Blessings, Queen Mother Dr. Delois Blakely